ALL DRESSED
DOWN
AND
NOWHERE
TO GO

ALL DRESSED
DOWN
AND
NOWHERE
TO GO

**CONTAINS THREE COMPLETE
DILBERT BOOKS:**

- Still Pumped from Using the Mouse (1996)
- Casual Day Has Gone Too Far (1997)
- I'm Not Anti-Business, I'm Anti-Idiot (1998)

A DILBERT® BOOK
BY SCOTT ADAMS

Andrews McMeel
Publishing

Kansas City

CASUAL DAY HAS GONE TOO FAR

A **DILBERT**® **BOOK** BY **SCOTT ADAMS**

DOGBERT EXPLAINS LEADERSHIP

LEADERS START THEIR CAREERS AS MORONS.

S. Adams

THEY ARE DRAWN TO MEETINGS LIKE MOTHS TO A PORCH LIGHT.

THE SUCCESSFUL MORON WILL HAVE A VERY HIGH BLADDER-TO-BRAIN RATIO.

BRAIN

BLADDER

THEY PREVAIL IN ALL DECISIONS BECAUSE THEY ARE IMPERVIOUS TO LOGIC OR COFFEE.

LET'S DO IT MY WAY!

OKAY!

© 1995 United Feature Syndicate, Inc.

THESE QUALITIES ARE PERCEIVED AS LEADERSHIP.

YOU'RE PROMOTED!

2-5

AFTER SEVERAL PROMOTIONS THEIR JOB TENDS TO MATCH THEIR TALENTS.

I AWARD YOU THIS AWARD.

CONCLUSION: LEADERSHIP IS NATURE'S WAY OF REMOVING MORONS FROM THE PRODUCTIVE FLOW.

9

RELIABLE SOURCES SAY YOUR PROJECT WILL BE CANCELLED, DILBERT.

2/20

YOU SHOULD ABANDON IT NOW AND COME WORK ON MY PROJECT. WHEN MY BIG PROMOTION GOES THROUGH NEXT MONTH, I'LL TRANSFER YOU TO MY GROUP AND GIVE YOU A RAISE.

THAT'S VERY TEMPTING EXCEPT FOR THE FACT YOU'RE A PATHOLOGICAL LIAR.

BE CAREFUL WHAT YOU SAY - I HAVE SUPER POWERS.

© 1995 United Feature Syndicate, Inc.

DOGBERT, I NEED YOUR HELP DEALING WITH A PATHOLOGICAL LIAR AT WORK.

2/21

YOU'RE IN LUCK. I HAPPEN TO HAVE A PH.D. IN LIATOLOGY FROM THE MASSACHUSETTS INSTITUTE OF TECHNOLOGY.

© 1995 United Feature Syndicate, Inc. (NYC)

I'D LOVE TO SEE YOUR DIPLOMA.

I'LL MAIL IT TO YOU.

WE'VE BEEN HAVING A PROBLEM WITH BLACK-OUTS. THE OFFICE LIGHTS ARE CONTROLLED BY MOTION DETECTORS.

I HIRED A TEMP TO WALK AROUND AND FLAP HIS ARMS SO THE LIGHTS WON'T GO OFF.

© 1995 United Feature Syndicate, Inc. (NYC)

ANOTHER JOURNALISM MAJOR ENTERS THE WORKFORCE.

IT SEEMS LIKE A WASTE. MAYBE HE COULD FAN US.

2/22

20

22

32

33

35

I'M GOING INTO BUSINESS AS A FINANCIAL ADVISOR.

SOUNDS HARD.

IT'S EASY. I'LL TELL ALL MY CLIENTS TO INVEST IN THE "DOGBERT DEFERRED EARNINGS FUND."

ISN'T THAT A CONFLICT OF INTEREST?

ONLY IF I SHOW INTEREST IN THE CLIENT.

DOGBERT: FINANCIAL ADVISOR

STOCKS... ANNUITIES... DERIVATIVES... CAPITAL GAINS TAX...

IT'S ALL TOO CONFUSING FOR YOU!! GIVE ME ALL YOUR MONEY NOW OR YOU'LL DIE A PAUPER!! NOW! NOW! BEFORE INTEREST RATES FALL!!

WILL THIS REDUCE MY INCOME TAXES?

MORE THAN YOU MIGHT GUESS.

DOGBERT: FINANCIAL ADVISOR

HERE'S A PICTURE OF YOU LIVING IN A DUMPSTER IN TWENTY YEARS.

BUT IF YOU INVEST IN THE "DOGBERT DEFERRED INCOME FUND" TAKE A LOOK AT WHAT YOU COULD OWN SOMEDAY!!

I COULD OWN A MANSION?!!

YOU COULD OWN A PHOTOGRAPH.

WE'RE MOVING TO A NEW OFFICE ACROSS TOWN. I VOLUNTEERED TO COORDINATE THE MOVE.

I CONTROL YOUR CUBICLE ASSIGNMENT. NAY, YOUR VERY EXISTENCE. FROM NOW ON YOU WILL REFER TO ME AS "LORD WALLY THE PUPPET MASTER."

I DON'T THINK IT'S LEGAL TO ENJOY YOUR WORK THIS MUCH.

I BANISH YOU TO THE CUBICLE CLOSEST TO YOUR BOSS!!

ALLOW ME TO INTRODUCE LOUD HOWARD.

HI!

I WILL MAKE LOUD HOWARD YOUR CUBICLE NEIGHBOR IN THE NEW OFFICE UNLESS YOU GIVE ME YOUR IMMORTAL SOUL!!

NICE DAY!

...FORTUNATELY I CONVINCED HIM TO TAKE MY LASER PRINTER INSTEAD...

WHAT DID I SAY THAT SOUNDED LIKE "TELL ME ABOUT YOUR DAY"?

"TO HEAR YOUR URGENT VOICE MAIL MESSAGE PRESS ONE..."

"THIS URGENT MESSAGE IS TO ALL EMPLOYEES. PLEASE DISREGARD THE RUMORS OF A MERGER WITH A HEALTHY COMPANY."

NOW SPOOKED, THE HERD STAMPEDES.

RÉSUMÉ!

WHERE'S MY INTERVIEW SUIT??!!

WE'VE GOT A LOT OF EMPTY CUBICLES BECAUSE OF DOWNSIZING.

I HIRED THE DOGBERT CONSTRUCTION COMPANY TO CONVERT PART OF THE OFFICE INTO PRISON CELLS WHICH WE'LL LEASE TO THE STATE.

SOUNDS LIKE A BIG JOB.

NAH. A LITTLE PAINT, NEW CARPET AND WE'RE THERE.

I DON'T THINK IT'S FAIR TO PUT CONVICTS IN OUR SPARE CUBICLES.

DON'T BE SUCH A BIGOT. THESE PEOPLE HAVE MADE ONE LITTLE MISTAKE. OTHERWISE, THEY'RE JUST LIKE EMPLOYEES.

I THINK THERE ARE A FEW DIFFERENCES!

YEAH, THEIR HEALTH PLAN IS BETTER.

HEY, BUDDY, WHAT ARE YOU IN FOR?

UNLIKE YOURSELF, I AM NOT A PRISONER HERE. I CHOOSE TO WORK HERE OF MY OWN FREE WILL!

GREAT... I'M IN THE FREAK SECTION.

I LIKE TO WORK.

EFFECTIVE IMMEDIATELY, WE WILL NO LONGER USE OUR SPARE CUBICLES TO HOUSE CONVICTS.

YES!!! OUR OPINIONS MATTERED!

ACTUALLY, IT'S BECAUSE THE PRISONERS COMPLAINED.

I WONDER WHAT HE PLANS TO DO WITH THE SPARE CUBICLES NOW.

BAD NEWS IN 1985

WE'RE REPLACING THE COMPANY DOCTOR WITH A REGISTERED NURSE.

BAD NEWS IN 1990

WE FIRED THE NURSE AND PUT THE ASPIRIN AND TOURNIQUETS IN THE VENDING MACHINE.

BAD NEWS IN 1995

WE'VE BEEN ASKED TO INCREASE VENDING MACHINE REVENUE BY FIFTEEN PERCENT.

I'M PLANNING TO TURN THE HOUSE INTO A GAMBLING CASINO.

ISN'T THAT ILLEGAL?

NOT IN THE TINY REPUBLIC OF DOGBERTLAND. I SECEDED FROM THE REPRESSIVE HOMELAND THIS MORNING.

I DON'T REMEMBER VOTING ON THAT.

HERE'S YOUR GREEN CARD.

40

THE **7** HABITS OF

HIGHLY DEFECTIVE PEOPLE

1. IGNORE ANY SIGNS OF DISCOMFORT IN OTHERS.

BUT HEY, I'VE BEEN DOING ALL OF THE TALKING.

2. USE HUMOR TO BELITTLE PEOPLE IN PUBLIC.

OUR NEWEST TEAM MEMBER HAS MOVIE STAR LOOKS. SPECIFICALLY, LASSIE.

3. TREAT ALL COMPLAINTS AS THE COMPLAINER'S FAULT.

YOU DON'T MOTIVATE ME.

MAYBE YOU SHOULD SEE A THERAPIST.

4. SHOW UP LATE AND RAISE CONTROVERSIAL ISSUES.

I THINK WE SHOULD LICENSE "BARNEY" AS OUR MASCOT.

5. GIVE ADVICE ON THINGS YOU DON'T UNDERSTAND.

TRY WRITING SOME ASSEMBLY LINE CODE HERE.

6. USE COMPLIMENTS TO SHOW YOUR PREJUDICES.

OOH, NICE CRISP PHOTO-COPY, ALICE. I DON'T THINK A MAN COULD HAVE DONE IT BETTER!

7. THINK THE COMICS ARE NOT ABOUT YOU

HEE HEE! LOOK AT THE HAIR ON THAT GUY!

WHO NEEDS TO SIGN MY BUSINESS CASE TO BUY A WEB SERVER?

HMM...THIS CROSSES ALL DEPARTMENTS. I FEAR IT. GET THE APPROVAL OF EVERY DIRECTOR, EVERY VP, EVERY EVP, PLUS GRIFFIN.

DO YOU MEAN TED GRIFFIN IN FINANCE OR THE MYTHICAL GRIFFIN BEAST THAT'S HALF EAGLE, HALF LION?

WHICHEVER IS HARDER.

I COULD GIVE YOU MARKETING'S APPROVAL RIGHT NOW...

OR I COULD FLEX MY VICE PRESIDENTIAL POWER AND SEND YOU TO GATHER MORE USELESS DATA... MY EGO WOULD EXPAND AND I'D BE A MAJOR STALLION WITH MY WIFE TONIGHT.

DO YOU THINK YOU CAN TOP THAT?

I'LL TRY, SIR. WHAT'S YOUR WIFE'S ADDRESS?

I NEED YOUR APPROVAL ON MY BUSINESS CASE, TOM.

I'LL WEDGE IT IN HERE SO YOU CAN CLAIM YOU NEVER SAW IT WHEN I ASK ABOUT IT NEXT WEEK.

THANKS

THE WEIRD PART IS THAT I CAN FEEL PRODUCTIVE EVEN WHEN I'M DOOMED.

5/15 © 1995 United Feature Syndicate, Inc. (NYC)

5/16 © 1995 United Feature Syndicate, Inc. (NYC)

5/17 © 1995 United Feature Syndicate, Inc. (NYC)

S. Adams

TODAY I DISTRIBUTED 36 COPIES OF MY BUSINESS CASE TO VARIOUS MANAGERS FOR APPROVAL.

BY MY COUNT, 20 ARE BEING MISPLACED, 6 MANAGERS WILL TRY TO KILL IT FOR PERSONAL GAIN AND 10 WILL COME BACK WITH IRRELEVANT QUESTIONS.

WHEN I DIE I WANT TO BE BURIED, NOT CREMATED, SO I CAN AT LEAST MAKE ONE LASTING IMPRESSION ON THE EARTH.

I WAS PLANNING TO MAIL YOUR CORPSE TO SOME- BODY I DON'T LIKE.

WE NEED TO BOOST OUR RETURN-ON- ASSETS RATIO.

LET'S ELIMINATE THE SECURITY DEPARTMENT. THAT WOULD CUT EXPENSES WHILE ALLOWING FOR A BRISK REDUCTION IN ASSETS.

WHEN ARE YOU PLANNING TO TELL HIM YOU WERE JOKING?

AFTER I FURNISH MY DEN.

YOU NEVER ANSWERED MY E-MAIL.

MY SECRETARY IS OUT, SO THERE'S NOBODY TO PRINT MY E-MAIL FOR ME. BRING ME YOUR MESSAGE ON HARDCOPY.

I WAS OUT OF PAPYRUS SO I CHISELED MY MESSAGE ON A LITTLE PYRAMID.

DID HE WORK ALONE OR WERE UFOs INVOLVED?

© 1995 United Feature Syndicate, Inc. (NYC) 5/18
© 1995 United Feature Syndicate, Inc. (NYC) 5/19
© 1995 United Feature Syndicate, Inc. (NYC) 5/20

S. Adams

50

OUR POLICY IS TO EMPLOY ONLY THE BEST TECHNICAL PROFESSIONALS.

QUESTION.

ISN'T IT ALSO OUR POLICY TO BASE SALARIES ON THE INDUSTRY AVERAGE?

RIGHT. WE LIKE THEM BRIGHT BUT CLUELESS.

I FEEL SORRY FOR PEOPLE LIKE THAT.

MY SALARY DEPENDS ON YOUR OPINION OF MY WORK. BUT YOU HAVE NO INTEREST IN UNDERSTANDING WHAT I DO, SO...

I HIRED THE DOGBERT PUBLIC RELATIONS FIRM TO HYPE MY PERFORMANCE AND GET ME A BIG RAISE

PRESS RELEASE: ENGINEER CURES CANCER WHILE SAVING BABY FROM BURNING BUILDING.

THAT'S NOT IN HIS OBJECTIVES.

YOU CAN CREATE THE ILLUSION THAT YOU WORK LONG HOURS BY LEAVING VOICE MAILS FOR YOUR BOSS AT 4 A.M.

HI, THIS IS DILBERT. IT'S 4 A.M. AND I'M IN MY UNDERWEAR AND I THOUGHT OF YOU... OOPS... ERASE... OOPS...

BEEP BEEP

DID YOU JUST SEND AN OBSCENE MESSAGE TO YOUR BOSS?

NO... I THINK I HIT THE GROUP CODE.

WHY DO YOU WANT TO TRANSFER TO MY DEPARTMENT, WALLY?

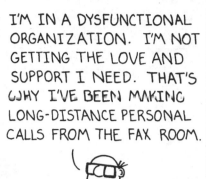

I'M IN A DYSFUNCTIONAL ORGANIZATION. I'M NOT GETTING THE LOVE AND SUPPORT I NEED. THAT'S WHY I'VE BEEN MAKING LONG-DISTANCE PERSONAL CALLS FROM THE FAX ROOM.

YOUR RÉSUMÉ SAYS EVERY BOSS YOU'VE HAD WAS A COMPLETE JERK.

SO, WHEN DO I START?

I HIRED RENOWNED PSYCHOLOGIST DOGBERT TO HELP US ACHIEVE PEAK PERFORMANCE IN TEAMWORK.

PEAK PERFORMANCE IS SOMEWHAT RELATIVE. YOU'RE A HIGHLY DYSFUNCTIONAL TEAM, SO WE MUST SET REALISTIC GOALS.

WHAT WOULD BE A REALISTIC GOAL FOR US?

I THINK I CAN POSTPONE CANNABILISM.

DYSFUNCTIONAL TEAM...

I'D LIKE EVERYBODY TO TURN TO THE RIGHT AND SAY WHAT YOU ADMIRE ABOUT THAT PERSON.

I ADMIRE YOUR LEATHERY SKIN, ALICE.

I ADMIRE YOUR ABILITY TO FIGURE OUT WHICH SIDE IS YOUR RIGHT IN ONLY TWO TRIES.

I ADMIRE YOUR ABILITY TO GET PAID FOR THIS.

DESPITE THE FACT YOUR FACE SCARES CHILDREN, I ADMIRE YOUR CO-WORKERS.

IN THIS TEAM-BUILDING EXERCISE YOU WILL MAKE PAPER DOLLS WHILE BLINDFOLDED.

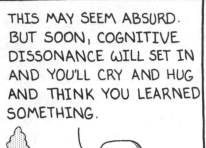

THIS MAY SEEM ABSURD. BUT SOON, COGNITIVE DISSONANCE WILL SET IN AND YOU'LL CRY AND HUG AND THINK YOU LEARNED SOMETHING.

ARE YOU SURE WE'LL CRY AND HUG?

ACTUALLY, HUGGING IS IFFY.

DYSFUNCTIONAL TEAM...

I'D LIKE EACH OF YOU TO TELL THE TEAM WHAT YOU LEARNED IN MY WORKSHOP.

I LEARNED TO LISTEN WITH MY HEART. I GAINED RESPECT FOR OTHERS. I UNDERSTAND SANSKRIT. I GOT MY HAM RADIO LICENSE. I CAN DIVIDE BY ZERO...

I LOVE GOING FIRST.

YOU'VE GOT TO INCREASE THE BUDGET FOR TRAINING!

IF I TRAIN YOU, THEN WOULDN'T YOU JUST LEAVE THE COMPANY TO MAKE MORE MONEY WORKING FOR OUR COMPETITOR?

I GUESS THERE IS A DOWN-SIDE.

AND THE DOWNSIDE WOULD BE...?

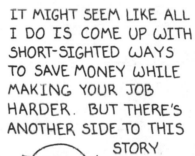

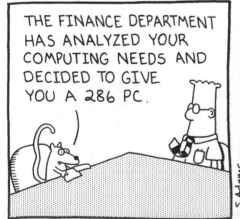

I RECOMMEND STANDARDIZING ON ONE TYPE OF COMPUTER FOR THE OFFICE.

WE MUST IDENTIFY AND ELIMINATE THE DEVIANT USERS OF MACINTOSH, UNIX AND... GOD HELP US... OS/2 WARP.

THE HOLY WARS BEGIN

DON'T LIE TO ME, GUSTAV! YOU'RE A STINKIN' MAC USER!!

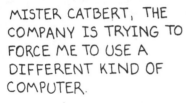

MISTER CATBERT, THE COMPANY IS TRYING TO FORCE ME TO USE A DIFFERENT KIND OF COMPUTER.

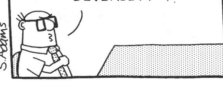

YOU'RE THE HUMAN RESOURCES DIRECTOR. WHAT ARE YOU DOING TO STOP THIS RELIGIOUS PERSECUTION??! WHAT EVER HAPPENED TO "DIVERSITY"??

THE LONGER YOU VERK HERE, DIVERSE IT GETS.

NEXT.

COMPUTER HOLY WARS

HOLD IT RIGHT THERE, BUDDY.

THAT SCRUFFY BEARD... THOSE SUSPENDERS... THAT SMUG EXPRESSION...

YOU'RE ONE OF THOSE CONDESCENDING UNIX COMPUTER USERS!

HERE'S A NICKEL, KID. GET YOUR-SELF A BETTER COMPUTER.

I JOKINGLY TOLD STAN IN MARKETING THAT I REPROGRAMMED HIS DNA. HE'S SO GULLIBLE THAT HE'S ACTUALLY CHANGING!

YOU MUST USE HIS GULLIBILITY TO REVERSE THE PROCESS. REMEMBER, HIS ENTIRE REALITY IS SHAPED BY UNVERIFIED CUSTOMER ANECDOTES.

I HEARD A RUMOR OF A STORY OF AN ALLEGED FOCUS GROUP WHERE A QUOTE TAKEN OUT OF CONTEXT INDICATES YOU'RE NOT BECOMING A WEASEL.

I'M NOT?!

YIPEEE!

OUR NEW DRESS POLICY AT WORK ALLOWS CASUAL CLOTHES ON FRIDAYS.

THAT'S GOOD, BECAUSE STUDIES HAVE SHOWN THAT FRIDAYS ARE THE ONLY SAFE DAY TO DRESS CASUALLY; ANY OTHER DAY WOULD CAUSE A STOCK PLUNGE.

IS IT JUST ME OR IS THAT POLICY STUPID?

THAT'S NOT AN "OR" QUESTION.

I WANT US TO HAVE THE SAME KIND OF TEAMWORK AS THE EGYPTIANS WHO BUILT THE PYRAMIDS!

SOME SCHOLARS BELIEVE THE PYRAMIDS WERE BUILT BY SLAVES.

BUT THERE'S SOME DOUBT; THAT'S ALL I'M SHOOTING FOR.

I THINK THEY WERE GUIDED BY UFOs TOO.

TED'S BABY SHOWER

OH LOOK, IT'S A STAPLER...

I CAN USE THIS TO TAKE UP THE HEM ON THE LOVELY HAND-CRAFTED PAPER BAG DRESS THAT DILBERT MADE.

IT LOOKS JUST LIKE THE ONE THAT DISAPPEARED FROM MY CUBICLE THIS MORNING.

EXCEPT YOURS HAD STAPLES.

IT'S REALLY DIFFERENT AROUND HERE SINCE WE LOST DILBERT'S DAD.

WHEN DID HE DIE?

HE'S NOT DEAD. WE LOST HIM AT THE MALL, CHRISTMAS OF '92.

SHOULDN'T YOU BE LOOKING FOR HIM?

I SAID IT'S DIFFERENT, NOT WORSE.

I CAN'T BELIEVE YOUR FATHER HAS BEEN LOST AT THE MALL SINCE 1992!

IF MY FATHER OR MY HUSBAND WERE LOST AT THE MALL I'D BE SEARCHING FOR HIM TWENTY-FOUR HOURS A DAY!!

WE'RE WAITING FOR A SALE.

YOU'RE A BIT OF A WHINER, AREN'T YOU, DEAR?

CONGRATULATIONS ON GETTING HIRED AS A TEMP, RATBERT.

WHERE DO I START?!

YOUR OFFICE IS THIS CARDBOARD BOX IN THE MAIN HALLWAY. THE REGULAR EMPLOYEES WILL NOT MAKE EYE CONTACT OR ASK YOUR NAME.

YOUR STATUS IS ROUGHLY BETWEEN THE SECURITY GUARD AND THE CRUD BEHIND THE REFRIGERATOR.

DO I GET A COMPANY CAR?

RATBERT THE TEMP WORKER

THIS IS REALLY TESTING MY SENSE OF SELF-WORTH.

I WILL COMPENSATE BY SHOUTING A LIST OF MY TALENTS TO ANYBODY WHO WALKS PAST.

IGNORE HIM. HE'S TRYING TO TRICK US INTO MAKING EYE CONTACT.

I EAT RUBBER! I CARRY DISEASE! I ENJOY OPERA!

RATBERT THE TEMP WORKER

I'M ONLY A TEMP, BUT I DEMAND RESPECT!!

OKAY, MAYBE THAT'S TOO MUCH TO ASK. BUT I DEMAND THAT SOMEBODY MAKE EYE CONTACT WITH ME!!

HOW'S THIS?

THAT'S PERIPHERAL VISION!!!

CATBERT THE HR DIRECTOR

I THINK I'LL INVENT SOME ILLOGICAL POLICIES TO ANNOY EMPLOYEES.

MY DIABOLICAL NEW DRESS CODE WILL MAKE THEM QUESTION THEIR OWN SANITY.

...SO, CASUAL CLOTHES DON'T LOWER OUR STOCK VALUE... BUT ONLY IF WORN ON FRIDAYS... UNLESS SOMEBODY SEES US... GOT IT?

I THINK I'M INSANE.

I DON'T UNDERSTAND YOUR NEW DRESS CODE POLICY, MR. CATBERT.

MAYBE YOU'RE INSANE.

IT'S SIMPLE. FRIDAYS ARE "CASUAL." BUT YOU CAN'T WEAR JEANS BECAUSE JEANS LOOK GOOD AND FEEL GOOD AND YOU ALREADY OWN SEVERAL PAIRS.

IT'S ANOTHER SADISTIC HUMAN RESOURCES PLOT TO MAKE PEOPLE QUIT!!

SAY HELLO TO UNSIGHTLY PANTY LINES.

WELL, IT WOULDN'T BE FRIDAY IF I DIDN'T SEE ALICE WEARING HER ONE PAIR OF TAN PANTS.

I LOVE THE "BUSINESS CASUAL" LOOK FOR THE WAY IT COMBINES UNATTRACTIVE WITH UNPROFESSIONAL WHILE DIMINISHING NEITHER.

DO YOU THINK THE FASHION OPINION OF A MALE ENGINEER MATTERS TO ME??

TWINS!

HERE'S HOW YOUR MARKETING DEPARTMENT CAN HELP RETAIN YOUR BEST ENGINEERS.

MARKETING GETS AN IDEA

WE'LL LEVERAGE OUR TECHNOLOGY BY BUILDING ANT FARMS.

SPREADSHEETS MAKE THE IDEA LOOK PROFITABLE.

THE ANT MILK ALONE WILL BE A POSITIVE NPV!

WHAT'S AN NPV?

WOW!

DON'T FORGET THE "WORST CASE SCENARIO."

WORST CASE, SOMEBODY BUILDS A GIGANTIC MAGNIFYING GLASS NEXT DOOR...

SOLUTION: BITE-SIZED ANT JERKY!

THERE'S NO RISK!

AN ENGINEER WILL BE ASSIGNED TO THE PROJECT.

ANT FARMS! DO IT!

UH-OH.

THE ENGINEER WILL CHALLENGE THE ASSUMPTIONS

YOU CAN'T GET A GALLON OF MILK FROM AN ANT!

WHAT DO YOU KNOW ABOUT MARKETING?

RESULT: THE ENGINEER WILL NEVER LEAVE THE COMPANY.

SO...YOUR CURRENT JOB IS "ANT FARM ENGINEER"?

I'M DOOMED.

8/13

MY STATUS FOR THE WEEK IS THAT THE ONGOING DEHUMANIZATION FROM MY JOB HAS CAUSED ME TO DOUBT MY EXISTENCE.

THERE IS REASON TO BELIEVE I AM BECOMING INVISIBLE.

DO I HEAR YOUR PAGER BUZZING, WALLY?

I DOUBT IT; I DON'T KEEP BATTERIES IN IT.

PLINK

THE DEHUMANIZATION OF MY JOB HAS RENDERED ME INVISIBLE TO HUMANS. ONLY YOU CAN SEE ME, DOGBERT.

HOW CAN WE FIX THIS?

YOU COULD WEAR A BAG ON YOUR HEAD WHEN YOU'RE AROUND ME.

THAT'S NOT THE FIX I HAD IN MIND.

IT'S NOT A PERFECT SOLUTION. I'D STILL BE ABLE TO HEAR YOU.

YOU'RE INVISIBLE TO YOUR CO-WORKERS. BUT YOU CAN COMPENSATE BY FORMING A SYMBIOTIC RELATIONSHIP WITH A VISIBLE CREATURE.

RATBERT WILL CLING TO YOUR BACK. HE'LL BE YOUR VISUAL AND AUDITORY LINK WITH YOUR CO-WORKERS.

SO... WORKING HARD? OR HARDLY WORKING?

I KNEW THIS COLOMBIAN COFFEE WAS TROUBLE.

DON'T BE ALARMED. I'M NOT REALLY A RAT FLOATING IN MIDAIR.

I'M CLINGING TO THE BACK OF AN EMPLOYEE WHO HAS BEEN RENDERED INVISIBLE BY A LONG SUCCESSION OF WORTHLESS ASSIGNMENTS.

LOOKS LIKE AN ISOLATED CASE OF BAD ATTITUDE.

WHICH ROOM IS THE "QUALITY" MEETING IN?

I SIGNIFICANTLY INCREASED MY VISIBILITY AT WORK TODAY, DOGBERT.

YESTERDAY I WAS INVISIBLE TO MY MANAGEMENT. BUT TODAY I AM KNOWN BY ALL.

YOU SCREWED UP, HUH?

OOH YEAH. BIG TIME.

I KNOW WHERE YOU'RE GOING.

YOU'RE GOING TO A MEETING WHERE EQUALLY UNINFORMED MANAGERS WILL MAKE DECISIONS THAT NEUTER THE WORK I DID ALL WEEK.

YOU DIDN'T DO ANY WORK THIS WEEK.

I THINK I'VE GOT THIS WHOLE "WORK" CONCEPT FIGURED OUT.

YOUR EXPENSE REPORT WAS REJECTED BY ACCOUNTING.

WHY?

BECAUSE THE EMPTINESS OF THEIR SHALLOW LIVES MAKES THEM WANT TO HURT OTHERS IN ORDER TO VALIDATE THEIR PATHETIC EXISTENCE.

CAN YOU HELP ME CLEAR THIS UP?

TO BE HONEST, I'M KINDA BUYING IN TO THEIR PHILOSOPHY.

IF IT'S OKAY, I'LL HOLD ONTO MY SOUL WHILE I VISIT THE ACCOUNTING DEPARTMENT.

SOUL CHECK

TIPS

I CAME TO ANSWER YOUR QUESTIONS ABOUT MY EXPENSE REPORT.

TAKE A SEAT.

I DON'T LIKE THE WAY THIS IS STARTING.

DILBERT'S EXPENSE VOUCHER

WHAT ARE YOU TRYING TO PULL?? DO YOU THINK WE'RE IDIOTS IN ACCOUNTING?!!

NO, I SWEAR, I THINK YOU'RE SMART BUT SADISTIC TROLLS WITH MANY HUMANOID CHARACTERISTICS.

APPARENTLY THERE WAS NO RIGHT ANSWER.

DILBERT'S EXPENSE VOUCHER

YOU SPENT NEARLY $10 PER DAY ON MEALS DURING YOUR TRIP.

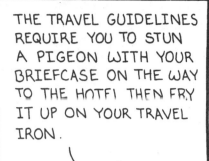

THE TRAVEL GUIDELINES REQUIRE YOU TO STUN A PIGEON WITH YOUR BRIEFCASE ON THE WAY TO THE HOTEL THEN FRY IT UP ON YOUR TRAVEL IRON.

I TRIED... BUT IT WAS TAKING SO LONG.

TRY THE "WOOL" SETTING.

DILBERT IS TRAPPED IN THE BOWELS OF ACCOUNTING

I UNDERSTAND YOU HAVE DILBERT IN THERE. FREE HIM, OR ELSE...

ELSE WHAT?

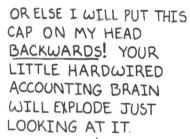

OR ELSE I WILL PUT THIS CAP ON MY HEAD BACKWARDS! YOUR LITTLE HARDWIRED ACCOUNTING BRAIN WILL EXPLODE JUST LOOKING AT IT.

WHAT WAS THAT POPPING SOUND?

A PARADIGM SHIFTING WITHOUT A CLUTCH.

SOMETIMES I FEEL SELF-CONSCIOUS BECAUSE MY BRAIN IS SO TINY.

HERE, LET ME REACH IN MY EAR AND PULL IT OUT.

I THINK THAT'S EAR WAX, BOB.

MAYBE. BUT I'M PUTTING IT BACK JUST IN CASE.

TINA, YOU'LL HAVE TO HAVE ALL THE DOCUMENTATION WRITTEN BY NEXT WEEK SO WE CAN SHIP IT WHEN THE SOFTWARE IS DONE.

HOW CAN I WRITE INSTRUCTIONS FOR SOMETHING THAT DOESN'T EXIST YET?

YOU'LL HAVE TO MAKE LOGICAL GUESSES.

"IF YOU PRESS ANY KEY YOUR COMPUTER WILL LOCK UP. IF YOU CALL OUR TECH SUPPORT WE'LL BLAME 'MICROSOFT.'"

I FEEL LIKE TWEAKING SOME BRITTLE PEOPLE. DO YOU KNOW ANY BRITTLE PEOPLE?

TRY TINA THE TECH WRITER. SHE BELIEVES THAT ALL FORMS OF EXPRESSION ARE AN INSULT TO HER GENDER AND HER PROFESSION.

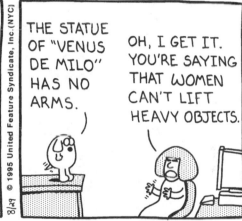
THE STATUE OF "VENUS DE MILO" HAS NO ARMS.

OH, I GET IT. YOU'RE SAYING THAT WOMEN CAN'T LIFT HEAVY OBJECTS.

DOGBERT TWEAKS TINA THE BRITTLE TECH WRITER.

WHAT DO YOU THINK OF THE MOVIE "THELMA AND LOUISE"?

I KNOW WHAT YOU'RE TRYING TO SAY. YOU THINK ALL WOMEN ARE BAD DRIVERS. THAT'S REALLY THE POINT OF THE MOVIE, ISN'T IT??

IF YOU'RE NOT OFFENDED YET, TUNE IN TOMORROW.

THE "THREE STOOGES"?

WHY ARE ALL OF THE DOCUMENTARIES ABOUT MEN??!

AS DIRECTOR OF HUMAN RESOURCES I'VE BEEN ASKED TO REDUCE THE COST OF EMPLOYEE BENEFITS.

THE COMPANY WILL NO LONGER PAY FOR EYE-GLASSES. BUT WE <u>WILL</u> SUPPORT A NEW VISION-CORRECTION PROCEDURE.

© 1995 United Feature Syndicate, Inc.(NYC)

RADIAL KERATOTOMY?

SQUINTING.

I HAVE TO CUT JANITOR EXPENSES. DO YOU THINK I'LL HAVE ANY HR ISSUES IF I MAKE EMPLOYEES EMPTY THEIR OWN TRASH?

WE'LL SOFTEN THE BAD NEWS BY SIMULTANEOUSLY INTRODUCING A NEW EMPLOYEE FITNESS PROGRAM...

OKAY, EVERYBODY, IT'S TIME TO TRASHERCISE!!!

I'M WRITING AN E-MAIL TO PROTEST THE NEW POLICY OF MAKING THE EMPLOYEES EMPTY THEIR OWN TRASH AT NIGHT.

IT'S STUPID TO HAVE HIGHLY PAID ENGINEERS DOING UNPRODUCTIVE TASKS WHEN WE COULD BE INVENTING THE FUTURE!

ARE YOU COMING TO THE "QUALITY FAIRE"?

NO, THIS WILL TAKE ANOTHER HOUR.

HERE'S THE PROBLEM. WE'VE GOT A WHOLE NEST OF PAPER TROLLS.

AAIIEE!

IF I CALL 911 NOW I'LL NEVER KNOW IF THE LOWER PAPER TRAY WOULD HAVE WORKED.

HERE'S MY TIME SHEET, FILLED OUT IN INCREMENTS OF FIFTEEN MINUTES.

AS USUAL, I CODED THE USELESS HOURS SPENT IN MEETINGS AS "WORK," WHEREAS THE TIME I SPENT IN THE SHOWER DESIGNING CIRCUITS IN MY MIND IS "NON-WORK."

INTERESTINGLY, EVEN THE TIME I SPEND COMPLAINING ABOUT MY LACK OF PRODUCTIVITY IS CONSIDERED "WORK."

I HATE MY LIFE.

IF THE DEPARTMENT MEETS ITS GOAL FOR THE QUARTER YOU CAN SHAVE MY HEAD!

THAT WOULD BE A BIG IMPROVEMENT.

HE'S TRYING TO SAVE MONEY ON A HAIRCUT

IF WE DOUBLE OUR GOAL CAN WE IRON YOUR SHIRT, TOO?

I NEED SOME LESS EXPERIENCED EMPLOYEES.

WHERE ARE YOU TAKING ALL OF THAT OFFICE EQUIPMENT?

I'M HAVING A GARAGE SALE.

OUR NEW COMPANY SLOGAN IS "ACT LIKE YOU OWN THE COMPANY." SO I'VE BEEN SELLING THE STUFF THAT I DON'T USE AND KEEPING THE MONEY.

IS THAT MY NEW COLOR MONITOR?

YEAH, I NEVER USED THAT THING.

I'M HAPPY TO REPORT THAT I HAVE EMBRACED THE NEW COMPANY SLOGAN "ACT LIKE YOU OWN THE COMPANY."

THIS MORNING I FIRED THE MARKETING DEPARTMENT AND HAD SECURITY ESCORT THEM OUT.

THAT'S NOT EXACTLY WHAT WE HAD IN MIND...

FORTUNATELY I ANTICIPATED YOUR REACTION.

PRESS "ONE" FOR SALES. PRESS "TWO" IN A HOPELESS EFFORT TO GET TECHNICAL SUPPORT.

PRESS "ONE" FOR ANSWERS TO QUESTIONS YOU DON'T HAVE. PRESS "TWO" IF YOU'RE GULLIBLE AND OPTIMISTIC.

PRESS "TWO" IF YOU'RE WILLING TO BUY SOMETHING JUST SO YOU CAN TALK TO A HUMAN BEING...

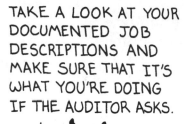

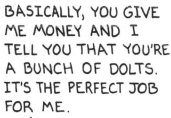

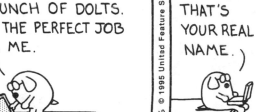

WE'RE POISED FOR SUCCESS. WE EXPECT HUGE EARNINGS AND INCREASED MARKET SHARE!

NEXT ON THE AGENDA... THERE WILL BE NO RAISES BECAUSE IT WILL BE A DIFFICULT YEAR...

CAROL, I THOUGHT I TOLD YOU TO PUT THE "UNITED WAY" UPDATE BETWEEN THOSE TWO AGENDA ITEMS.

OOPSIE.

YOUR RÉSUMÉ DOESN'T LIST ANY EXPERIENCE AS A JET PILOT, MISTER DOGBERT.

HOW HARD COULD IT BE?

YOU COULD SPEND A LOT OF MONEY ON SOME PRETTY BOY PILOT WITH EXPERIENCE, OR YOU CAN SAVE A FEW BUCKS AND HAVE ME DRIVE THE CORPORATE JET.

I AM UNDER A LOT OF BUDGET PRESSURE... AND I'M NOT ALLOWED ON THE JET MYSELF...

IT HAS A PILOT EJECT SEAT, RIGHT?

DOGBERT, CORPORATE JET PILOT

ATTENTION, PASSENGER.

I'M CAPTAIN DOGBERT. THIS IS MY FIRST FLIGHT. I'LL BET YOU WISH YOU HADN'T CUT THE CORPORATE TRAINING BUDGET.

FOR SAFETY, KEEP AN EYE OUT THE WINDOW... IF IT LOOKS LIKE WE'RE GONNA HIT THE GROUND, TRY JUMPING UP RIGHT BEFORE IMPACT.

WELCOME TO HEAVEN, MISTER DOGBERT.

WOW, IT LOOKS LIKE YOU GUYS RELAXED YOUR STANDARDS!

DOGS ARE AUTOMATIC. NO MATTER WHAT YOU DO, THERE'S ALWAYS A PLACE IN HEAVEN FOR EVERY LITTLE DOG.

I'D LIKE THAT BACK NOW, IF YOU DON'T MIND!!

WHAT KIND OF DISTANCE CAN YOU GET WITH THESE LITTLE "FRISBEES"?

MISTER DOGBERT, WE'VE DECIDED TO SEND YOU BACK TO EARTH AS AN ANGEL.

YOUR MISSION IS TO HELP PEOPLE IN NEED. WE HAVE GIVEN YOU SPECIAL POWERS.

WE'LL BE WATCHING.

OKAY, SO WHAT'S THE PRICE FOR NEW HAIR PLUS BUNS OF STEEL?

AHEM

IT'S ALL ON THE PRICE SHEET.

ARE YOU SAYING THAT YOU'RE AN ANGEL NOW? AND YOU HAVE SPECIAL POWERS TO HELP PEOPLE.

EXACTLY. I INSTINCTIVELY KNOW WHAT PEOPLE WANT AND I CAN GIVE IT TO THEM WITH A SNAP OF THE PAW.

SNAP

ARE YOU HAVING ANY TROUBLE CONTROLLING IT?

MY AIM STINKS.

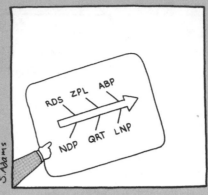

WE'VE DECIDED TO REVOKE YOUR ANGEL STATUS. YOU'RE GIVING US ALL A BAD NAME.

YOUR PROBLEM IS THAT YOU DEFINE "HEALING" TOO NARROWLY. I'M MAKING UGLY PEOPLE LOOK ATTRACTIVE, AND THAT'S IMPORTANT, TOO.

IS IT TOO LATE TO GO BACK TO MY OLD LOOK?

WHY? YOU'RE BEAUTIFUL!

CAROL, ABOUT THIS FLIGHT TO NEW YORK THAT YOU BOOKED FOR ME...

IS IT REALLY NECESSARY TO MAKE ALL THESE STOPOVERS IN THIRD-WORLD COUNTRIES THAT ARE EXPERIENCING REBEL INSURRECTIONS?

YOU'D BETTER WEAR THE INTERNATIONAL SYMBOL OF THE "RED CROSS" ON YOUR BACK.

TERRIBLE NEWS: MY BOSS ASSIGNED ME TO A FUN AND VALUABLE PROJECT.

UH-OH. THAT MEANS AT LEAST THREE MORONS WILL BE ASSIGNED TO SIMILAR PROJECTS. YOU MUST FIND THEM AND CRUSH THEM...

EXACTLY.

CARL, OLD BUDDY, WHATCHA WORKIN' ON THESE DAYS?

NOTHING FUN AND VALUABLE. SHOO SHOO!!

117

WALLY AND I HAVE A BET ABOUT WHY YOU ASSIGNED ME TO THE SAME TASK AS THREE OTHER PEOPLE.

I BELIEVE IT'S A CLEVER PLOY TO CREATE HEALTHY INTERNAL COMPETITION. WALLY THINKS YOU'RE JUST DUMBER THAN THE AVERAGE CAULIFLOWER.

MAY I POINT OUT THAT CAULIFLOWER IS THE BRAIN OF THE FRUIT KINGDOM.

YES!

THREE OTHER PEOPLE ASKED FOR THAT SAME INFORMATION. YOU MUST BE ON REDUNDANT PROJECTS.

HERE'S A BIG BINDER WHICH AT FIRST GLANCE SEEMS USEFUL, BUT YOU'LL REALIZE LATER IT'S NOT.

I'VE GOT A FEW MORE USELESS BINDERS. DO YOU WANT 'EM?

SURE. I'M USING THEM TO BUILD AN ADDITION TO MY CUBICLE.

IT LOOKS LIKE SOMEBODY IS USING BINDERS TO ILLEGALLY INCREASE THE SIZE OF HIS CUBICLE.

YOU THINK YOUR STATUS WILL INCREASE WITH YOUR CUBICLE SIZE, DON'T YOU! WELL, IT WON'T WORK!

HERE'S A RAISE. I DON'T KNOW WHY.

PSSST. IS HE SEEING ANYBODY?

RRRR

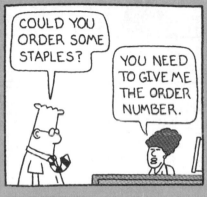

119

I HEARD YOU GOT ASSIGNED ON A "DOTTED LINE" TO OUR BOSS' ARCH-RIVAL.

GROAN

LOOK ON THE BRIGHT SIDE. THINK OF YOURSELF AS LEADING THE EXCITING LIFE OF A SECRET DOUBLE-AGENT!

DON'T MOST DOUBLE-AGENTS GET CAPTURED AND EXECUTED IMMEDIATELY?

THEY WISH IT WAS IMMEDIATE.

THE "DOGBERT CORPORATE ART SOURCE" WILL PROVIDE LOW-COST PAINTINGS FOR YOUR WALLS.

OUR MOTTO IS "IF IT'S IN A FRAME IT WILL LOOK LIKE ART TO YOU."

HOW MUCH DO THE PAINTINGS COST?

SIX DOLLARS A POUND.

HOW DID YOU GET THE CONTRACT TO SUPPLY OUR COMPANY WITH WALL ART?

LOW BID.

AS WE SPEAK, MY ASSISTANT IS SCOURING THE EARTH IN SEARCH OF LOW-COST ART.

SCHOOL-O-ART

I'LL TAKE IT!!

121

123

SAINT DOGBERT ENTERS THE LAND OF CUBICLES SEARCHING FOR THE DEMONS OF STUPIDITY.

SUDDENLY HE FINDS AN OVER-PROMOTED COMPUTER GURU SPOUTING USELESS DATABASE CONCEPTS.

YOU'D BE FOOLS TO IGNORE THE BOOLEAN ANTI-BINARY LEAST-SQUARE APPROACH.

THE MONSTER IS DISPATCHED TO THE DARK WORLD BY THE SIGHT OF ITS MOST FEARED OBJECT.

LOOK! ACTUAL CODE!

COOL!

SSSS SSS

HOW LONG WILL IT TAKE TO FIX ANY PROBLEMS WE FIND IN OUR BETA PRODUCT?

IT IS LOGICALLY IMPOSSIBLE TO SCHEDULE FOR THE UNKNOWN.

TRY TO THINK AS A MANAGER, NOT AS AN ENGINEER.

IN THAT CASE, WE'LL FIX THE PROBLEMS BEFORE WE FIND THEM.

THIS NEXT TRANSPARENCY IS AN INCOMPREHENSIBLE JUMBLE OF COMPLEXITY AND UNDEFINED ACRONYMS.

YOU MIGHT WONDER WHY I'M GOING TO SHOW IT TO YOU SINCE THE ONLY POSSIBLE RESULT IS TO LOWER YOUR OPINION OF MY COMMUNICATION SKILLS.

FRANKLY, IT'S BECAUSE I LIKE MAKING COMPLEX PICTURES MORE THAN I LIKE YOU.

S. Adams

© 1995 United Feature Syndicate, Inc. (NYC)

I'M NOT ANTI-BUSINESS, I'M ANTI-IDIOT

A DILBERT® BOOK
BY SCOTT ADAMS

Blah, blah, blah, Pam. Blah, blah, blah.

Introduction

I'm a misunderstood cartoonist.

The people who misunderstand me the most are the ones who write to tell me they enthusiastically agree with my opinions. Those people scare me. Sometimes they develop irrational attractions to me, based on the fact that our opinions are so similar. They often inquire about the possibilities of mating with me, or—if they are male—drugging me and keeping me in a basement in a big glass container. It's all very flattering.

Other people write to tell me they plan to hunt me down and beat me senseless with ceramic statues because my opinions are at odds with their own well-constructed views of the universe. The people who worship unicorns come to mind. They're a vindictive group.

Still other people call me a hypocrite because their incomplete information about my actions is inconsistent with their misinterpretation of my opinions. I deal with this the only way I know how to—by signing their names to anti-unicorn literature.

The problem with other people's opinions about my opinions is that no one actually knows my opinions. All anyone knows about me is the dialogue I put in the mouths of rotund engineers, talking rats, megalomaniac dogs, and pointy-haired bosses. I might be dumb, but I'm not dumb enough to express my true opinion about anything important. The one thing I've learned about freedom of expression is that you really ought to keep that sort of thing to yourself.

That said, I do feel an irrational need to make one futile attempt to clear up the biggest misconception about my opinions: I'm not anti-*management*. I'm anti-*idiot*. The two groups intersect so often that I use the terms interchangeably, even though I know I shouldn't. Let me set the record straight: If you think you're a smart manager, you have my word that I'm only making fun of other people.*

Sincerely,

S.Adams

Scott Adams

*Unless you worship unicorns.

THE COMPANY HAS DECIDED TO OUTSOURCE ALL OF THE FUNCTIONS THAT WE'RE NOT ANY GOOD AT.

Yippee! Yay!

WHEN'S YOUR LAST DAY?

UH-OH...THEY'RE NOT GOOD AT KNOWING WHAT THEY'RE NOT GOOD AT...

© 1995 United Feature Syndicate, Inc.(NYC) 11/23

I DON'T UNDERSTAND WHY SOME PEOPLE WASH THEIR BATH TOWELS.

WHEN I GET OUT OF THE SHOWER I'M THE CLEAN-EST OBJECT IN MY HOUSE. IN THEORY, THOSE TOWELS SHOULD BE GETTING CLEANER EVERY TIME THEY TOUCH ME.

MAYBE I COULD HUG YOU EVERY DAY SO I DON'T NEED TO TAKE SHOWERS.

ARE TOWELS SUPPOSED TO BEND?

© 1995 United Feature Syndicate, Inc. (NYC) 11/24

I'VE GOTTA RUN TO THE POST OFFICE.

YOU GO TO THE POST OFFICE EVERY DAY. ARE YOU AWARE THAT YOU CAN BUY MORE THAN ONE STAMP AT A TIME?

APPARENTLY YOU DON'T UNDERSTAND THE CONCEPT OF "FLOAT."

© 1995 United Feature Syndicate, Inc. (NYC) 11/25

S.Adams

MY PASSWORD FOR THE NETWORK ISN'T WORKING

FILL OUT A A HELP REQUEST ONLINE.

I CAN'T GET ONLINE BECAUSE MY PASSWORD DOESN'T WORK...

SEND ME AN E-MAIL MESSAGE ABOUT IT.

I CAN'T SEND E-MAIL BECAUSE I CAN'T GET ON THE STINKIN' NETWORK !!!

GEEZ, YOU'RE WORTHLESS...

DOES HUMAN RESOURCES OFFER ANY TREATMENT PROGRAMS FOR PEOPLE WITH DYSFUNCTIONAL INTERNET CONNECTIONS?

I RECOMMEND THE "YARN THERAPY." YOU'LL BE WRAPPED IN A HUGE BALL OF YARN AND USED AS FURNITURE IN MY OFFICE.

IS THIS LIKE THE FAMOUS "ROPES" COURSE WHERE I LEARN TO SOLVE PROBLEMS AS PART OF A TEAM?

EXACTLY, EXCEPT HERE YOU LEARN TO BE MY COUCH.

ALICE, DID YOU HEAR THAT DILBERT'S NETWORK CONNECTION ISN'T WORKING?

UH-OH

HE IS WHAT WE CALL A TECHNOLOGY "HAVE NOT." HIS COMPETITIVENESS IN THE GLOBAL ECONOMY WILL LAST AS LONG AS THIS FRENCH FRY.

SO SAD.

AFTER LUNCH, I'M GOING TO USE SOMETHING CALLED "ELECTRONIC MAIL." YOU CAN WATCH IF YOU PROMISE NOT TO TOUCH ANY-THING.

SNORK!

GULP

ON ONE HAND, MY COMPANY DOES USE INFERIOR TECHNOLOGY IN OUR PRODUCTS...

BUT ON THE OTHER HAND, I'M THE MOST ATTRACTIVE FEMALE WHO HAS PAID ATTENTION TO YOU THIS YEAR.

WHAT KIND OF ENGINEERS DO YOU THINK WE ARE??!

DO YOU HAVE PICTURES OF YOUR FIELD SUPPORT PEOPLE?

I CAN'T BELIEVE YOU'RE RECOMMENDING THIS LOUSY VENDOR JUST BECAUSE THE SALES REP IS GORGEOUS.

HERE'S A PICTURE OF THOR, THEIR FIELD ENGINEER.

DOES HE REALLY WORK WITHOUT A SHIRT?

ONLY IF YOU BUY THE "INDIAN CHIEF" MAINTENANCE PACKAGE.

YOUR EMPLOYEES HAVE RECOMMENDED A VENDOR WHO HAS AN ATTRACTIVE SALESPERSON.

BUT THE "DOGBERT TECHNOLOGY COMPANY" CAN PROVIDE YOU WITH A HARDWARE SOLUTION FOR HALF THE COST!

I'LL SAVE MONEY!

WHAT IF I NEED TO UPGRADE LATER? IS IT EXPENSIVE?

I MUST HAVE LEFT THAT PRICE SHEET IN MY OTHER FUR.

SO, YOU IGNORED MY RECOMMENDATION AND BOUGHT A LOW-COST SYSTEM THAT'S TOTALLY INADEQUATE...

YOU COMPENSATED FOR THIS BLUNDER BY MAKING IT PART OF MY OBJECTIVES TO MAKE THE SYSTEM WORK...

YOU'LL GET A BONUS FOR SAVING MONEY. I'LL GET FIRED, THUS SAVING MORE MONEY AND EARNING YOU ANOTHER BONUS.

I'M ON A ROLL.

IT'S FUNNY — BEFORE YOUR COMPANY BOUGHT THAT CRITICAL SYSTEM FROM ME, YOU HAD ALL THE POWER...

BUT NOW, ONLY I CAN PROVIDE ESSENTIAL UPGRADES!! I CALL THE SHOTS, YOU SIMPLE FOOL!!

SEND IN THE NEXT EMPLOYEE.

AT LEAST WE DON'T HAVE ANY MULTI-VENDOR COMPATIBILITY ISSUES.

IT'S INEXPLICABLE, BUT THE LOW-COST SYSTEM I SOLD YOU SEEMS TO BE WOEFULLY UNDER-POWERED.

YOU COULD REPLACE IT WITH ANOTHER VENDOR'S SYSTEM, THUS SHOWING EVERYBODY YOU MADE A MISTAKE. OR YOU CAN PAY MY OUTRAGEOUS UPGRADE FEES.

HOW BIG A FOOL DO YOU THINK I AM?

I WON'T KNOW UNTIL I SEE IF YOU GO FOR THE LEASE OPTION.

S. Adams

© 1995 United Feature Syndicate, Inc. (NYC)

143

WAIT-A-MINUTE... I'M STARTING TO REALIZE SOMETHING.

MY JOB TITLE IS SENIOR ASSOCIATE, YET I SPEND MY TIME DOING CLERICAL WORK... AND UNLESS I'M MISTAKEN, I'M THE LOWEST PAID EMPLOYEE.

IS THIS A BAD TIME?

AAAGH!! I'M A SECRETARY!

I READ SOMEWHERE THAT CERTAIN RELIGIONS REQUIRE THEIR INITIATES TO PERFORM POINTLESS NEVER-ENDING TASKS TO RID THEM OF THEIR EGOS.

WHAT NOW?

WHEN I CONQUER THE WORLD I'LL HAVE A SECRET HANDSHAKE TO IDENTIFY THE PEOPLE WHO WILL BE PART OF MY NEW RULING CLASS.

CROSS YOUR EYES AND STICK OUT YOUR TONGUE. GOOD, NOW VIGOROUSLY SLAP YOUR FACE.

THE PEOPLE WHO AREN'T DOING THAT WILL BE IDENTIFIED AS MY NEW RULING CLASS.

SLAP!

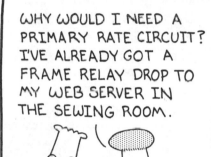

149

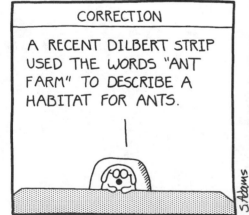

153

Panel 1: I PROMOTED TED TO BE YOUR NEW MANAGER. I USED TO THINK HE LOOKED BOYISH, BUT HIS NEW BEARD CHANGED THAT.

Panel 2: ARE EITHER OF YOU THE LEAST BIT CONCERNED THAT TED'S BEARD IS GROWING FROM HIS FOREHEAD?

Panel 3: SHE MADE IT SOUND AS IF IT'S WRONG.

YOU CAN PUNISH THEM FOR HAVING BAD OPINIONS.

Panel 4: AS YOUR NEW BOSS I HAVE YET TO SELECT MY "PET" EMPLOYEE. I SHALL DO THIS BY CLOSING MY EYES AND POINTING THE BEARD ON MY FOREHEAD.

Panel 5: TO MAKE IT FAIR, I'LL CLOSE MY EYES WHILE ONE OF YOU SPINS MY CHAIR!

Panel 6: ALICE...UM... TECHNICALLY THIS ISN'T "SPINNING."

STAIRS

Panel 7: HOW DO YOU LIKE BEING A MANAGER, TED?

Panel 8: YESTERDAY MY STAFF PUSHED ME DOWN TEN FLIGHTS OF STAIRS. MY SOUL LEFT MY BODY AND NOW I'M A LIFELESS EVIL ENTITY.

Panel 9: JUST IN TIME TO DO PERFORMANCE REVIEWS!

I COULDN'T HAVE PLANNED IT BETTER.

DOGBERT MEETS WITH SOFTWARE DEVELOPERS

NOTE THE HUGE MARKET FOR SOFTWARE THAT RUNS ON THE "DOGBERT 2000" OPERATING SYSTEM.

BUT WHO CARES? THE IMPORTANT THING IS THAT I BROUGHT A BAG OF TOYS.

SOME SAY THE COMPUTER INDUSTRY IS BUILT ON SILICON. I THINK FOAM AND PLASTIC ARE EQUALLY IMPORTANT.

THANKS TO MY SOFTWARE EMPIRE, MY NET WEALTH IS TWENTY BILLION DOLLARS.

CONTRARY TO POPULAR OPINION, IT DOES SEEM TO MAKE ME HAPPY.

MONEY CAN'T BUY A SUNSET, DOGBERT.

NO, BUT I WAS ABLE TO LICENSE THE DIGITAL RIGHTS.

I HEARD YOU WERE DOING SOME BABY-SITTING, BOB.

YEAH! I DID THE MORTON TRIPLETS LAST NIGHT.

IT'S NOT EASY TO JUGGLE THREE SCREAMING TODDLERS.

IT'S THE MORTONS WITH A QUESTION ABOUT THEIR CEILING FAN.

WHEN YOU SAY "JUGGLE"...

THE COMPANY ANNOUNCED A NEW COMPENSATION PLAN TODAY. BONUSES WILL BE PAID ONLY TO THE TOP TEN PERCENT OF THE EMPLOYEES.

IN RELATED NEWS, 89% OF THE EMPLOYEES RESIGNED IN BITTER DISGUST. THE TOP TEN PERCENT ALSO LEFT, REALIZING THEY COULD GET BETTER JOBS ELSE-WHERE.

THIS COULD HAVE AN IMPACT ON THOSE OF YOU WHO REMAIN.

WE GET THE BONUSES?

I'M INVENTING A NEW TECHNOLOGY TO PREVENT KIDS FROM SEEING SMUT ON THE INTERNET.

SO, YOU'RE PITTING YOUR INTELLIGENCE AGAINST THE COLLECTIVE SEX DRIVE OF ALL THE TEENAGERS WHO OWN COMPUTERS?

WHAT IS YOUR POINT?

DID YOU KNOW THAT IF YOU PUT A LITTLE HAT ON A SNOWBALL IT CAN LAST A LONG TIME IN HELL?

MATT, YOUR JOB IS TO TEST MY NEW INVENTION THAT BLOCKS KIDS FROM SEEING DIRTY PICTURES ON THE INTERNET.

HIS YOUTHFUL CURIOSITY IS NO MATCH FOR MY TECHNICAL BRILLIANCE.

I HOPE THAT WASN'T THE SOUND OF EYEBALLS GETTING REALLY BIG.

I'VE ASKED DOGBERT TO HELP US GET RID OF OUR MOST TROUBLESOME CUSTOMERS.

GRRR

TEN PERCENT OF YOUR CUSTOMERS ACCOUNT FOR NINETY PERCENT OF YOUR SERVICE COSTS. THEY MUST BE ELIMINATED.

IS THAT THE SAME GROUP OF CUSTOMERS WHO ACTUALLY USE OUR PRODUCT?

PLUS THE ONES WHO WERE INJURED UNPACKING IT.

I'VE REDUCED YOUR SERVICE COSTS BY GIVING THE TECHNICAL-SUPPORT GROUP AN UNLISTED PHONE NUMBER.

AND A FLAW IN YOUR PRODUCT DISABLES THE CUSTOMER'S E-MAIL; THEY CAN'T EVEN WRITE TO YOU FOR HELP!

WHAT IF THEY ASK A FRIEND TO E-MAIL US?

PEOPLE WHO USE OUR PRODUCT DON'T HAVE FRIENDS.

REALLY? I USE IT.

...BUT OUR PRIMARY VENDOR CAN'T DELIVER, SO...

I WONDER WHAT'S ON TV TONIGHT.

...SHOULD WE RISK A LAWSUIT OR BUILD A PRODUCT THAT NOBODY ON EARTH WANTS?

DID HE ASK ME TO MAKE A CHOICE?

WILL IT BE A REQUEST FOR INFORMATION OR AN IMPRACTICAL SOLUTION?

LET'S DO BOTH!

WE WON THE BID TO REBUILD OUR NATION'S AIR TRAFFIC CONTROL SYSTEMS.

YIPPEEE!!!

YES!!

TO THE PHONES!

THEY DON'T USUALLY GET THAT EXCITED.

BUY A THOUSAND SHARES OF "BLUEHOUND BUS LINES."

I HIRED THE "DOGBERT CONSULTING COMPANY" TO LEAD THE PROJECT BECAUSE NONE OF YOU IS BRIGHT ENOUGH.

AND YOU ALL HAVE BAD ATTITUDES FOR NO APPARENT REASON; THAT'S NO WAY TO BE A LEADER.

SHALL WE GO AROUND THE TABLE AND INTRODUCE OURSELVES?

I DON'T GET CHUMMY WITH THE LOCALS.

WALLY WRITES THE CRITICAL CODE FOR OUR NATION'S NEW AIR TRAFFIC CONTROL SYSTEM.

THE CROWD IS SILENT.

SUDDENLY THE GIFTED PROGRAMMER EMPLOYS A RARELY SEEN STRATEGY OF "CODE REUSE."

THE CROWD GOES WILD.

SO YOU USED CODE FROM THE PAYROLL SYSTEM?

HERE'S A TIP: DON'T FLY ON PAY DAY.

THANKS TO MY LEADER-SHIP, THE NEW AIR TRAFFIC CONTROL SYSTEM IS DESIGNED ON TIME AND UNDER BUDGET.

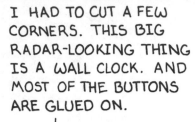

I HAD TO CUT A FEW CORNERS. THIS BIG RADAR-LOOKING THING IS A WALL CLOCK. AND MOST OF THE BUTTONS ARE GLUED ON.

IT LOOKS LIKE IT MIGHT BE UM... DANGEROUS.

GREAT... I FINISH EARLY AND WHAT DO I GET: "FEATURE CREEP."

I NEED EVERYBODY TO HELP IN THE SHIPPING DEPART-MENT TODAY.

EVERY PRODUCT THAT SHIPS BEFORE THE END OF THE MONTH GETS COUNTED AS REVENUE FOR THE FISCAL YEAR. UNFORTUNATELY, WE DON'T HAVE INVENTORY.

SO WE'LL SHIP WHATEVER IS LYING AROUND, BOOK IT AS REVENUE AND SORT IT OUT LATER.

THIS ONE'S GETTING GUM.

HEY, WALLY! THE BOSS SENT HIS FIRST E-MAIL MESSAGE!

AND YOU SAID HE WASN'T BRIGHT ENOUGH TO FIGURE OUT HOW TO USE E-MAIL!

WHAT'S HIS MESSAGE?

"I FORGOT MY WATCH. DOES ANYBODY KNOW WHAT TIME IT IS?"

TIME TO CHANGE JOBS.

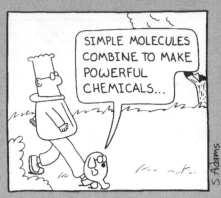

HERE'S THE REVISED STANDARD EMPLOYMENT AGREEMENT. SIGN IT OR BE FIRED.

"THIS AGREEMENT IS BETWEEN THE COMPANY (HEREAFTER REFERRED TO AS 'THE ONLY COMPANY THAT WOULD EVER HIRE YOU') AND YOU (HEREAFTER CALLED 'PUDDING HEAD')."

IT SEEMS TO HAVE A BIT OF ATTITUDE.

OUR LAWYERS TURNED ON US. I SUSPECT RABIES.

I CAN'T BELIEVE THEY EXPECT US TO SIGN THESE NEW EMPLOYMENT AGREEMENT FORMS.

ACCORDING TO THIS, ANYTHING WE EVEN THINK OF BECOMES THE COMPANY'S PROPERTY. I'M SURPRISED THEY DON'T CLAIM OUR FIRSTBORN SONS!

WHAT DO YOU SUPPOSE IT MEANS WHEN THEY COPYRIGHT OUR "DNA AND ALL DERIVATIVE WORKS"?

THEY'D MAKE AN EXCEPTION FOR YOU.

LOOK AT THE AGREEMENT MY COMPANY IS FORCING US TO SIGN. THEY CLAIM THE RIGHTS TO ANY IDEA AN EMPLOYEE EVER HAS.

NO PROBLEM. JUST RETYPE IT WITH A FEW STRATEGIC OMISSIONS AND SIGN IT. THEY CAN'T PROOFREAD EVERY ONE.

WOULDN'T THAT BE DISHONEST?

MAYBE YOU COULD JUST SHOW THEM SOME OF YOUR IDEAS AND THEY'D GRANT A WAIVER.

2/15/96 © 1996 United Feature Syndicate, Inc.(NYC)

2/16/96 © 1996 United Feature Syndicate, Inc.(NYC)

2/17/96 © 1996 United Feature Syndicate, Inc.(NYC)

SOMEWHERE IN ELBONIA

I'VE BEEN ASSIGNED TO CHECK THE SOFTWARE YOU'RE WRITING FOR US UNDER CONTRACT.

THE DOCUMENTATION IS WRITTEN IN OUR OWN ELBONIAN LANGUAGE.

IS THAT A PROBLEM?

THAT'S BETTER THAN I'D HOPED. I WAS AFRAID NOBODY HERE KNEW HOW TO WRITE.

WRITING IS EASY. SOMEDAY WE HOPE TO READ, TOO.

BEFORE I ACCEPT THE SOFTWARE YOU WROTE UNDER CONTRACT, TELL ME WHAT DEVELOPMENT METHODOLOGY YOU USE.

WE HOLD VILLAGE MEETINGS TO BOAST OF OUR SKILLS AND CURSE THE DEVIL-SPAWNED END-USERS.

SOMETIMES WE JUGGLE.

AT THE LAST MINUTE WE SLAM OUT SOME CODE AND GO ROLLER SKATING.

I WOULD FIND THIS HUMOROUS IF NOT FOR THE PIG ON MY BACK.

YOU SAVED ONE MILLION DOLLARS BY HAVING PROGRAMMERS IN ELBONIA WRITE SOFTWARE FOR US.

BUT WE WASTED FOUR MILLION DOLLARS TRYING TO DEBUG THE SOFTWARE.

AND THE ENTIRE STAFF OF OUR QUALITY ASSURANCE GROUP QUIT TO BECOME MIMES.

LET'S BLAME THE MIMES; THEY WON'T TALK.

DOGBERT, I NEED YOU TO FACILITATE SOME MEETINGS.

WHAT KIND OF MEETINGS?

WE'RE CREATING A PROCESS TO FIX OUR PRODUCT DEVELOPMENT PROCESS. BUT FIRST WE'RE HAVING SOME PREPLANNING MEETINGS...

...TO DECIDE ON A PROJECT NAME.

HOW ABOUT "DEATH SPIRAL"?

I'VE BEEN ASKED TO FACILITATE THIS MEETING. I ALONE WILL DETERMINE WHO CAN SPEAK.

I'D LIKE TO BEGIN WITH A RAW DISPLAY OF MY POWER. YOU MAY NOT SPEAK.

HEY, WALLY... DID YOU EVER HEAR OF A THING CALLED EXERCISE?

I THINK YOU'LL AGREE THAT THIS MEETING WENT SMOOTHLY WITH ME AS FACILITATOR.

THE BREAKTHROUGH WAS WHEN I REALIZED I WAS THE ONLY ONE HERE WITH ANYTHING VALUABLE TO SAY.

LET'S HAVE A MOMENT OF SILENCE TO HONOR ME FOR MY BRILLIANT WORK DESPITE BEING SURROUNDED BY DOLTS.

179

ADD AN EXECUTIVE SUMMARY TO THE APPROVAL PAGE.

KEEP IT SIMPLE. OUR EXECUTIVES DON'T UNDERSTAND AS MUCH ABOUT TECHNOLOGY AS I DO.

HOW COULD THEY KNOW LESS THAN YOU DO? YOU HAVEN'T FIGURED OUT HOW TO MAKE YOUR CAR GO UPHILL.

WRONG; I GOT AAA ROAD SERVICE.

I HAVE TO TURN THIS FIFTY-PAGE PROPOSAL INTO A ONE-PARAGRAPH EXECUTIVE SUMMARY FOR OUR CEO. IT'S IMPOSSIBLE.

SIMPLE.

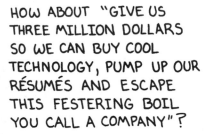

HOW ABOUT "GIVE US THREE MILLION DOLLARS SO WE CAN BUY COOL TECHNOLOGY, PUMP UP OUR RÉSUMÉS AND ESCAPE THIS FESTERING BOIL YOU CALL A COMPANY"?

I FEEL OBLIGATED TO SAY SOMETHING ABOUT OUR CUSTOMERS.

HOW ABOUT "I'M GLAD I'M NOT ONE OF THEM."

COULD YOU DO A DEMO OF THE NEW PRODUCT FOR OUR VP NEXT WEEK?

WELL... THAT WOULD DELAY THE SHIP DATE, LOWER MORALE AND CREATE AN UNENDING DEMAND FOR MORE UNPRODUCTIVE DEMOS...

LOGICALLY, SINCE YOUR OBJECTIVE IS TO SHOW THAT WE'RE DOING VALUABLE WORK...

AND WE'LL NEED A BANNER THAT SAYS "QUALITY."

181

182

RATBERT, WE'D LIKE YOU TO BE THE DIRECTOR OF MARKETING FOR THE COMPANY WE'RE STARTING.

OKAY! WHAT DO I DO?

BE AS ANNOYING AND ILLOGICAL AS YOU CAN. WE'LL WHACK YOU IN THE HEAD WITH BALLED-UP SOCKS TO MAKE YOU SHUT UP.

IT'S DEFINITELY BETTER TO BE AN OWNER THAN AN EMPLOYEE.

LET'S LINK HIS SALARY TO EARNINGS! HEE HEE!

THE BUSINESS PLAN FOR YOUR START-UP IS IDIOTIC BUT I'M GOING TO PROVIDE THE VENTURE CAPITAL FUNDING ANYWAY.

WE'LL GENERATE LOTS OF MEDIA HYPE, GO PUBLIC AND MAKE MILLIONS BY SHAFTING GREEDY AND IGNORANT INVESTORS.

THE LATIN WORD FOR "CLOSE YOUR EYES AND OPEN YOUR MOUTH" IS "PROSPECTUS."

THIS IS EXACTLY WHY I'M AFRAID OF DOGS.

WALLY AND I STARTED OUR OWN COMPANY. WE'RE SELLING THE PRODUCT THAT YOU SAID NOBODY WANTS.

SOON WE WILL BE RICH.

WE DO OUR VICTORY JIG IN YOUR FACE.

BA-BUM

WHEN HE SHOWED YOU YOUR EMPLOYMENT AGREEMENT — WHERE YOU GAVE ALL PATENT RIGHTS TO THIS COMPANY — WHAT PART OF THE JIG WERE YOU DOING?

TURBO MOONING.

SOB

I HAVE AN ETHICAL QUESTION, DOGBERT.
I'M HERE TO HELP.
S. Adams
IS IT BETTER TO GIVE CUSTOMERS A LOW QUALITY PRODUCT IN A TIMELY FASHION...
OR IS IT BETTER TO LIE ABOUT PRODUCT AVAILABILITY UNTIL THE BUGS ARE FIXED?
I WILL NEED MY ASSISTANT, RATBERT, TO ADDRESS YOUR ETHICAL QUESTION.
SNAP
LET'S SAY RATBERT IS A TRUSTING AND INNOCENT CUSTOMER.
© 1996 United Feature Syndicate, Inc.(NYC)
3/17/96
SUPPOSE SOMEBODY ABUSES HIS TRUST LIKE THIS...
SMACK
HOW DOES THIS RELATE TO MY SITUATION?
TO BE HONEST, I WASN'T LISTENING TO YOU.

AT THE RISK OF DYING FROM BOREDOM, I MUST INTERVIEW YOU FOR THE DEPARTMENT NEWSLETTER.

LET ME GIVE YOU SOME BACKGROUND BEFORE I TALK ABOUT MY PROJECT...

"THE PROJECT IS GOOD," QUIPPED THE ENGINEER.

...SO THERE I AM IN MY MOM'S FALLOPIAN TUBE...

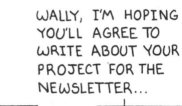

WALLY, I'M HOPING YOU'LL AGREE TO WRITE ABOUT YOUR PROJECT FOR THE NEWSLETTER...

AND IN THE GRAND TRADITION OF ENGINEERING, I EXPECT YOU'LL GIVE THIS THE LOWEST PRIORITY, THUS MAKING ME DESPISE YOU.

SO... ARE YOU SAYING YOU DON'T DESPISE ME NOW?

WE ARE NOT HAVING A "MOMENT" HERE!

PERFORMANCE REVIEW

YOUR MAIN ACCOMPLISHMENT WAS THE DEPARTMENT NEWSLETTER WHICH WAS BOTH UNINTERESTING AND UNIMPORTANT. YOU GET NO RAISE.

THE NEWSLETTER WAS YOUR IDEA, AND IT'S BORING BECAUSE MOST OF THE ARTICLES ARE CONTRIBUTED BY MY IDIOTIC COWORKERS.

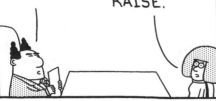

YOU DON'T SEEM TO UNDERSTAND THE VALUE OF TEAM-WORK.

I UNDERSTAND ITS VALUE; IT JUST COST ME A TWO-PERCENT RAISE.

Panel 1: IN AN EFFORT TO BOOST SALES, LAPTOP COMPUTERS HAVE BEEN GIVEN TO EVERY MEMBER OF THE SALES FORCE.

Panel 2: THAT COULD BE A PROBLEM, GIVEN THE RECENT CUTS TO THE TRAINING BUDGET.

Panel 3: MEANWHILE, IN THE FIELD

AND IF YOU ORDER TODAY, I'LL THROW IN THIS RECTANGULAR PLASTIC THING.

Panel 4: I WISH I HAD AN IVY LEAGUE DEGREE SO I COULD BE PROMOTED TO VICE PRESIDENT.

YOU DON'T NEED ONE.

Panel 5: IT'S IMPOSSIBLE TO BE A VICE PRESIDENT WITHOUT ONE.

I'LL BET $100 I CAN TURN A RAT INTO A VICE PRESIDENT.

Panel 6: THAT WAS GOOD, BUT TRY SAYING IT AS THOUGH YOUR SOUL JUST ABANDONED YOUR BODY.

"WE'VE REORGANIZED TO FOCUS ON OUR CORE COMPETENCY."

Panel 7: REMEMBER EVERYTHING I TAUGHT YOU, RATBERT. IF YOU CAN PASS YOURSELF OFF AS A CORPORATE VICE PRESIDENT, I'LL WIN MY BET.

Panel 8: YO, HEADCOUNT! IF YOU HAVE ANY ISSUES, PUT TOGETHER AN ACTION PLAN. OUR PEOPLE ARE THE BEST. DON'T SPEND MONEY.

Panel 9: DO YOU THINK HE'S REALLY A VICE PRESIDENT?

MAYBE. BUT I'M NOT READY TO RULE OUT "ANNOYING RODENT" YET.

QUALITY.

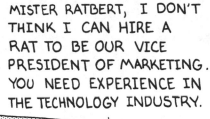

MISTER RATBERT, I DON'T THINK I CAN HIRE A RAT TO BE OUR VICE PRESIDENT OF MARKETING. YOU NEED EXPERIENCE IN THE TECHNOLOGY INDUSTRY.

I SPENT A WEEK IN A DUMPSTER AT PROCTER AND GAMBLE.

CLOSE ENOUGH! WELCOME TO THE TEAM!

I'LL BRING SOME CRONIES WITH ME. THEY'RE FLIES.

I HAD YEARS OF VALUABLE EXPERIENCE AS A RODENT BEFORE I BECAME VICE PRESIDENT OF MARKETING.

MY MARKETING PLAN IS SIMPLE. EACH OF YOU WILL CLING TO THE LEG OF A TECHNOLOGY COLUMNIST UNTIL WE GET SOME GOOD PRESS.

IT LOOKS LIKE YOU'RE FULL.

YOU CAN CLING TO THE CAT UNTIL A SPACE OPENS.

I QUIT MY JOB AS VICE PRESIDENT OF MARKETING...

I WAS LOSING MY SCRUPLES... BECOMING UNSCRUPULOUS. YES, I LEARNED A VALUABLE LESSON ABOUT SCRUPLES.

AND THAT LESSON WOULD BE?

IT'S FUN TO SAY "SCRUPLES."

TODAY WAS A BAD DAY. FIRST THE VENDING MACHINE STOLE MY MONEY...

...AND BY THE END OF THE DAY I HAD BEEN SENTENCED TO DEATH BY THE DIRECTOR OF HUMAN RESOURCES...

I'VE BECOME TOTALLY DESENSITIZED TO TRAGIC NEWS!

THE EXECUTION IS SCHEDULED FOR TOMORROW. I SHOULD CALL IN SICK.

DOGBERT VERSUS CATBERT

I UNDERSTAND YOU'VE SENTENCED DILBERT TO DEATH.

IS THAT A PROBLEM?

MY ASSISTANT, BOB THE DINOSAUR, WILL NOW DEMONSTRATE HOW TO GIVE A CAT A "FUR WEDGIE."

I'VE BEEN PARDONED. SOMEHOW THEY LOST THE PAPERWORK ORDERING MY EXECUTION.

IT PROBABLY FELL INTO A CRACK.

THE INTERNAL JOB POSTINGS ARE OUT. HERE'S A JOB I'D LOVE.

"EXPERIENCE REQUIRED: THE CANDIDATE MUST BE A GUY NAMED ERIC, POT-BELLIED, NEARSIGHTED, MUST DRIVE A RED FORD BRONCO."

THEY MIGHT HAVE SOMEONE IN MIND ALREADY.

IF I SQUINT... AND LEAVE MY "CONTROL TOP" PANTYHOSE AT HOME...

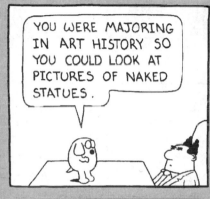

ALICE, YOU'VE BEEN WORKING EIGHTEEN HOURS A DAY. I REALIZED I MUST ADD A PERSON TO THE EFFORT.

SO I HIRED A NIGHT SHIFT MANAGER. AFTER I GO HOME AT FIVE O'CLOCK HE'LL TAKE OVER AND ASK WHY YOU'RE BEHIND SCHEDULE.

I LIKE MY STATUS REPORTS RENDERED IN 3-D, BUT DON'T SPEND A LOT OF TIME ON IT.

THIS DOG IS SPECIALLY TRAINED TO DETECT WASTED RESOURCES.

HE'LL HELP ME FIND OUT WHY YOUR PROJECT IS BEHIND SCHEDULE EVEN AFTER ADDING ME AS MANAGER.

SNIFF SNIFF

WE'LL BEGIN AS SOON AS HE'S DONE PLAYING AROUND.

OH MY! THIS IS SHOCKING!

WHAT?

40% OF ALL SICK DAYS TAKEN BY YOUR STAFF ARE FRIDAYS AND MONDAYS!

WHAT KIND OF IDIOT DO THEY THINK I AM?

NOT AN IDIOT SAVANT. THEY CAN DO MATH.

CATBERT, H.R. DIRECTOR

WALLY, IT MIGHT NOT SEEM FAIR THAT NEW EMPLOYEES ARE PAID MORE THAN YOU...

BUT YOU COULD ALWAYS QUIT AND THEN REAPPLY FOR YOUR OLD JOB AT A HIGHER SALARY.

I JUST MIGHT DO THAT!!

WOULD YOU MIND RUBBING THIS CATNIP ALL OVER YOUR BODY FIRST?

SO I'M THINKING I'LL RESIGN, THEN I'LL REAPPLY FOR MY CURRENT JOB AT A HIGHER SALARY.

THAT'S A GOOD PLAN EXCEPT FOR THE FACT THAT YOU'RE THOROUGHLY UNQUALIFIED FOR YOUR CURRENT JOB.

I NEED TO SHARE MY UNREALISTIC PLANS WITH A FRIEND WHO ISN'T AN ENGINEER.

I'M MORE OF A CO-WORKER THAN A FRIEND, PER SE.

AND THAT'S THE MARKETING PLAN. ANY COMMENTS?

IT APPEARS TO BE A BUNCH OF OBVIOUS GENERALITIES AND WISHFUL THINKING WITH NO APPARENT BUSINESS VALUE.

MARKETING DIDN'T TURN OUT TO BE THE GLAMOUR CAREER I EXPECTED.

I CIRCLED ALL THE WORDS YOU WON'T FIND IN ANY DICTIONARY.

 EXPERIMENT #1: I AM EXPOSING A RAT TO MY COMPANY'S MARKETING PLAN.

 HE SEEMS TO HAVE NO ADVERSE RESPONSE TO THE INTRODUCTION AND BACKGROUND.

 THIS IS ALREADY FAR MORE EXPOSURE THAN HUMANS COULD TOLERATE.

SALES PROJECTIONS...
BRAIN TUMOR...
GET TYLENOL...

 HERE'S MY TIME SHEET, INCLUDING GUESSES FOR THE NEXT TWO DAYS SO I CAN MEET YOUR ARBITRARY CLERICAL DEADLINE.

 IF ANYTHING IMPORTANT COMES UP, I'LL IGNORE IT TO PRESERVE THE INTEGRITY OF THE TIME-REPORTING SYSTEM.

 ARE YOU FINISHED ANNOYING ME YET?

ACCORDING TO MY TIME SHEET I'LL BE HERE FOR ANOTHER 14 MINUTES.

 I GOT MYSELF A LITTLE WORK-AVOIDANCE DEVICE.

 IF I WANT TO LEAVE A MEETING EARLY, I JUST LOOK DOWN AND SAY "UH-OH" AND SCURRY AWAY.

 WHAT'S THE PAGER NUMBER IN CASE I NEED YOU?

YOU'RE NOT QUITE GRASPING THE CONCEPT HERE, ALICE.

CATBERT, H.R. DIRECTOR

I'VE COME TO GIVE YOU "EMPLOYEE ORIENTATION," WALLY.

BUT I'VE WORKED HERE FOR YEARS.

YOU STILL HAVE A GLIMMER OF HOPE. YOU'LL HAVE TO WATCH THIS MANDATORY TRAINING VIDEO.

SO, YOU STILL HAVE HOPE...

RELAX... LET IT GO.

I'M PLEASED TO REPORT ANOTHER BANNER WEEK OF ACCOMPLISHMENTS!

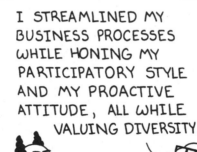

I STREAMLINED MY BUSINESS PROCESSES WHILE HONING MY PARTICIPATORY STYLE AND MY PROACTIVE ATTITUDE, ALL WHILE VALUING DIVERSITY!

YOU WATCHED THE MANDATORY TRAINING VIDEOS?

AND I LOST MY FREE WILL!

I JUST WATCHED THE MANDATORY VIDEO ON SEXUAL HARASSMENT. IT WORKED!

IN ONLY THIRTY MINUTES, THAT VIDEO CORRECTED A BILLION YEARS OF EVOLUTION. DO SOMETHING SEXY AND WATCH ME IGNORE IT!

I PROBABLY SHOULDN'T HAVE FAST-FORWARDED THROUGH THE BORING PARTS.

204

THIS WEEK I KICKED OFF THE "WALLY COMPENSATION EQUILIBRIUM PROJECT."

MY GOAL IS TO LOWER THE QUALITY OF MY WORK UNTIL IT IS CONSISTENT WITH MY SALARY.

I HATE THE FIRST MONTH AFTER THEY SEE THEIR RAISES.

I'D GO ON, BUT I JUST ACHIEVED EQUILIBRIUM.

CATBERT, THE EVIL DIRECTOR OF HUMAN RESOURCES

WE'RE MOVING TO "CAFETERIA STYLE" BENEFITS.

UNDER THIS SYSTEM, IF YOU NEED HEALTH CARE, YOU WANDER THROUGH THE CAFETERIA ASKING "DOES ANYBODY KNOW WHAT THIS RED LUMP IS?"

WHAT IF IT'S A LIFE-THREATENING PROBLEM?

THAT REMINDS ME, THE CAFETERIA WON'T BE LABELING THE ENTREES ANYMORE.

I'M GOING TO TRY MY PAW AT BEING A CAREER COUNSELOR.

INSECURE PEOPLE WILL SEEK MY ADVICE AND I'LL TELL THEM TO BE MORE SELF-RELIANT.

THAT SOUNDS LAZY AND UNHELPFUL.

WOULD YOU WANT CAREER ADVICE FROM SOMEBODY WHO HAS TO WORK HARD?

DOGBERT, CAREER COUNSELOR

YOU CAN'T EXPECT YOUR EMPLOYER TO TAKE CARE OF YOU FOREVER, WALLY.

DON'T EXPECT RAISES, DON'T EXPECT TO BE TRAINED AND DON'T EXPECT A PENSION.

THAT'S DEPRESSING. I NEED A SOURBALL.

THOSE ARE MARBLES WRAPPED IN CELLOPHANE.

DOGBERT, CAREER COUNSELOR

ACCORDING TO YOUR OCCUPATIONAL PREFERENCE TEST, YOU LIKE TO REMOVE VITAL ORGANS FROM HELPLESS PEOPLE.

THAT NARROWS THE CAREER CHOICES TO DOCTOR OR SERIAL KILLER. DO YOU GET ALONG WITH OTHER PEOPLE?

OTHER PEOPLE ARE INSIGNIFI-CANT INSECTS.

WE'LL HAVE TO GO TO A TIE-BREAKER QUESTION.

DOGBERT, CAREER COUNSELOR

I'M A LOWLY TECHNICAL WRITER NOW, BUT MY GOAL IS TO BECOME A FAMOUS NOVELIST.

MY PLAN IS TO WRITE WITTY AND SCATHING E-MAIL MESSAGES ABOUT CO-WORKERS UNTIL A PUBLISHER GIVES ME AN ADVANCE.

THEY MIGHT EXPECT YOU TO WRITE A BOOK AT SOME POINT.

BLOOD SUCKERS!

THE COMPANY ANNOUNCED WE'RE BEING BOUGHT BY OUR LONG-TIME RIVAL.

DON'T WORRY ABOUT LAYOFFS. THEY LIKE ENGINEERS. IN FACT, THEY ALREADY HAVE A DIVISION THAT DOES WHAT WE DO!

EXCEPT THEY'RE YOUNGER AND THEY AREN'T PAID AS MUCH AS WE ARE...

SPIN

AFTER THE MERGER, WE'LL REDUCE STAFF IN AREAS THAT ARE REDUNDANT.

I HOPE THE EMPLOYEES OF THIS COMPANY WILL BE EVALUATED FAIRLY COMPARED TO THOSE IN THE BUYING COMPANY.

WE ALREADY HAVE A BALD GUY.

DOES YOURS STEAL OFFICE FURNITURE, TOO?

I'M PARALYZED WITH FEAR BECAUSE OF THE PENDING MERGER.

THANKS TO YOUR LEADERSHIP I'VE GONE FROM BEING UNMOTIVATED TO BEING INERT.

I THINK I'M ADVANCING TO THE NEXT PHASE. HELLO, RIGOR MORTIS!! TAKE ME, I'M READY!!

IT MIGHT BE TIME FOR A MORALE-BOOSTING POTLUCK LUNCH.

IN THE "DUE DILIGENCE" PHASE OF OUR MERGER YOU WILL GIVE US ACCESS TO ALL OF YOUR PROPRIFTARY INFORMATION.

WOULDN'T THAT LET YOU KNOW HOW TO CRUSH US COMPETITIVELY? COULDN'T YOU CANCEL THE MERGER AND TAKE OUR CUSTOMERS WITHOUT PAYING A CENT?

MUST...CONTAIN MANIACAL...LAUGH...

"DUE DILIGENCE" BEFORE THE MERGER.

YOU MUST REVEAL YOUR SECRETS SO MY COMPANY KNOWS WHAT IT'S BUYING.

ALL OF OUR PROJECTS ARE DOOMED. MOST OF THE GOOD EMPLOYEES LEFT. OUR CUSTOMERS ARE STARTING A CLASS ACTION SUIT...

AT LEAST THE BUILDING IS WORTH SOMETHING

IF YOU FEEL A TICKLE, THAT'S ASBESTOS.

WITH ALL THIS TALK OF "DIVERSITY" THERE'S NO MENTION OF THE PAIN WE SMART CREATURES ENDURE WHILE SURROUNDED BY DOLTS.

GOOD POINT. I DON'T KNOW HOW WE DO IT.

IT LOOKS LIKE I'LL HAVE TO HOLD SECRET MEETINGS.

YEAH, OUR LIVES ARE A CONSTANT STRUGGLE.

BUSINESS LANGUAGE EXPLAINED

S. Adams

"WE HAVE TO BE MORE COMPETITIVE."

NICE BARREL.

THIS OLD THING?

MEANING: SAY GOODBYE TO SALARY INCREASES.

"WE MUST FOCUS ON OUR CORE BUSINESS."

HELLO.

MEANING: WE CAN'T FIND OUR BUTTS WITH BOTH HANDS.

"YOU ARE EMPOWERED."

I PROCLAIM THIS TO BE "GREEN INK DAY."

MEANING: YOU'RE THE MONARCH OF UNIMPORTANT DECISIONS.

"WE'RE REENGINEERING YOUR FUNCTION."

MEANING: ADIOS, TONTO, AND THE HORSE YOU RODE IN ON.

"TRAINING IS ESSENTIAL."

YOU WERE A CANNIBAL?

I'M A PEOPLE PERSON.

MEANING: WE'RE TRYING TO HIRE SOME TRAINED PEOPLE.

"WE'RE MARKET DRIVEN."

WHAT'S YOUR FAVORITE ODOR?

RESEARCH

MEANING: WE BLAME CUSTOMERS FOR OUR LACK OF INNOVATION.

"WE VALUE EMPLOYEE INPUT."

THANKS FOR LISTENING.

HA HA HA!

MEANING: WE THINK HUMOR IS IMPORTANT.

5/26/96

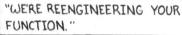

216

TORMENTING THE VENDOR

YOU MUST DO OUR BIDDING, VENDOR. WE CONTROL YOUR ECONOMIC FUTURE.

OF COURSE, OUR BUYING DECISION WILL BE BASED SOLELY ON QUANTIFIABLE PERFORMANCE MEASUREMENTS.

YOUR COMPETITOR COMPLETED THE "VENDOR CHALLENGE COURSE" IN 37 SECONDS.

AND HE GAVE US VERY NICE T-SHIRTS.

DILBERT, I FOUND YOUR FATHER. HE'S BEEN AT THE "ALL YOU CAN EAT" RESTAURANT IN THE MALL SINCE 1989.

HE'S SO LITERAL— HE DIDN'T WANT TO LEAVE UNTIL IT WAS "ALL HE COULD EAT."

WHEN'S HE COMING HOME?

I'M THINKING OF JOINING HIM. HE GOT A BOOTH.

I CAN'T BELIEVE YOUR FATHER HAS BEEN LIVING IN THE "ALL YOU CAN EAT" RESTAURANT SINCE 1989!

YOU HAVE THE ODDEST FAMILY. WHAT DID HE LOOK LIKE WHEN YOU SAW HIM AFTER ALL THESE YEARS?

I HAVEN'T SEEN HIM YET. I'M WAITING FOR "BURRITO NIGHT."

NOW IS WHEN YOU SHOULD BE SAYING "JUST KIDDING."

OUR OBJECTIVES ARE UNCLEAR AND OUR MISSION STATEMENT IS GIBBERISH...

BUT THANKS TO AN ARTIFICIAL SENSE OF URGENCY, I'M WORKING HARDER THAN EVER!

WHAT'S THE GOOD NEWS YOU SAID YOU HAVE?

APPARENTLY I'M INSANE. BUT I'M ONE OF THE HAPPY KINDS!

THIS COMPANY MAKES PERFECT SENSE, NOW THAT I'M INSANE.

FOR EXAMPLE, IT MIGHT SEEM AS THOUGH WE'RE WOEFULLY UNDERSTAFFED, BUT I CAN COMPENSATE BY WORKING SMARTER NOT HARDER.

HEY, IF I'M CAPABLE OF WORKING SMARTER, THEN WHY DO I WORK HERE?

THE HEALING HAS BEGUN.

DILBERT, I NOTICE YOU'VE BEEN LOOKING DEPRESSED LATELY.

HERE'S A PRESCRIPTION FOR AN ANTIDEPRESSANT DRUG. BE SURE TO EXERCISE REGULARLY AND DON'T SKIP MEALS.

WHAT MAKES YOU THINK YOU'RE QUALIFIED TO DIAGNOSE MY MENTAL HEALTH?!!

I'D BETTER DOUBLE IT.

223

CAROL, I ASKED YOU TO ENROLL ME IN THE QUALITY COLLEGE, BUT THE CONFIRMATION SAYS CLOWN COLLEGE.

IT'S A PREREQUISITE COURSE.

THIS IS GONNA COST ME ON SECRETARIES DAY.

I HOPE IT'S OKAY TO BE AN ANGRY CLOWN.

I WAS GOING TO GET THE "BUNS OF STEEL" VIDEO BUT I'M MAKING EXCELLENT PROGRESS WITHOUT IT.

WHEN THEY SAY STEEL, IT REFERS TO HARDNESS, NOT WEIGHT.

I KNEW IT SEEMED TOO EASY.

STAY AWAY FROM LARGE MAGNETS.

THE ONLY EMPLOYEE SUGGESTIONS THAT GET ACCEPTED ARE THE ONES THAT ARE HARMLESS AND STUPID.

I SUBMITTED SOME HARMLESS AND STUPID IDEAS TO TEST MY THEORY.

SUGGESTION: REPLACE ALL #2 PENCILS WITH #4 PENCILS. THE HARD LEAD LASTS LONGER YET COSTS THE SAME.

THAT COULD WORK.

HERE'S A DRAFT OF MY NEW OBJECTIVES. I TRIED TO MAKE THEM ACHIEVABLE.

"NO MATTER HOW STUPID MY CO-WORKERS ARE, I WILL NOT PUNCH A HOLE IN ANYONE'S TORSO, RIP OUT A VITAL ORGAN AND KEEP IT IN MY CUBICLE AS A WARNING TO OTHERS."

I HOPE SHE GETS THOSE OBJECTIVES APPROVED.

YES! IT'S MEASURABLE!

I COULD SIT HERE DOING NOTHING.

OR I COULD IMPLEMENT A BOLD QUALITY INITIATIVE WITH THE HELP OF MY TALENTED AND ENERGETIC COWORKERS.

I CRACK ME UP.

WHAT EXACTLY IS THE DOGBERT DAY CARE CONCEPT?

PROGRESSIVE COMPANIES CAN PROVIDE DAY CARE WITHOUT SPENDING A BUNDLE.

WOULDN'T WE SPEND A FORTUNE ON DUCT TAPE?

IT'S REUSABLE UNLESS IT GETS SLOBBERED ON.

RATBERT, MY COMPANY IS HIRING FOR OUR QUALITY ASSURANCE GROUP. YOU'D BE PERFECT.

WHAT WOULD I HAVE TO DO?

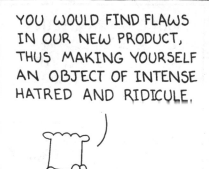

YOU WOULD FIND FLAWS IN OUR NEW PRODUCT, THUS MAKING YOURSELF AN OBJECT OF INTENSE HATRED AND RIDICULE.

BUT THEN YOU'D FIX THOSE FLAWS... AND YOUR RESPECT FOR ME WOULD GROW INTO A SPECIAL BOND OF FRIENDSHIP, RIGHT?!

NO, THEN WE SHIP.

I'D BE PERFECT FOR THE JOB IN QUALITY ASSURANCE. HERE'S MY RESUME.

ARE YOU BOTHERED BY THE FACT THAT HALF OF YOUR WORDS ARE SPELLED WRONG?

NOPE! I'M NOT EVEN BOTHERED BY YOUR ANAL RETENTIVE BEHAVIOR.

YOU'RE HIRED. YOUR BONUS WILL EQUAL NEGATIVE 100% OF YOUR BASE SALARY. OKAY?

I DON'T SEE ANY PROBLEM WITH THAT.

MY QUALITY ASSURANCE REVIEW OF YOUR BETA PRODUCT TURNED UP A FEW BUGS, WALLY.

I'VE CLASSIFIED THE BUGS BY SEVERITY: 1) LETHAL, 2) BONEHEADED, 3) VEXING.

ALL I SEE ARE LETHAL AND VEXING. WHERE'S BONEHEADED?

I'M TRYING TO RENT A STADIUM TO HOLD THE PRINTOUT.

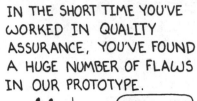

IN THE SHORT TIME YOU'VE WORKED IN QUALITY ASSURANCE, YOU'VE FOUND A HUGE NUMBER OF FLAWS IN OUR PROTOTYPE.

THAT'S MY JOB!

YOU'RE JEOPARDIZING OUR SCHEDULE. THE ENTIRE PROJECT WILL FAIL AND IT'S ALL <u>YOUR</u> FAULT.

WHY IS IT <u>MY</u> FAULT?

IF A TREE FALLS IN THE FOREST... AND WE'VE ALREADY SOLD THE TREE... DOES IT HAVE QUALITY?

HOW MANY ANGELS CAN DANCE ON YOUR HEAD?

LET'S HAVE A LITTLE PREMEETING TO PREPARE FOR THE MEETING TOMORROW.

WHOA! DO YOU THINK IT'S SAFE TO JUMP RIGHT INTO THE PREMEETING WITHOUT PLANNING IT?

OKAY, LET'S GET THIS PRELIMINARY PREMEETING MEETING GOING.

YOU THINK YOU'RE FUNNY, BUT YOU'RE NOT.

I COULDN'T HELP NOTICING THE BUGS IN THE PROGRAM ON THIS OLD DISKETTE YOU THREW AWAY.

I FIXED THE BUGS AND TIGHTENED THE CODE FROM TWELVE THOUSAND LINES TO SIXTEEN.

IT TOOK ME THREE MONTHS TO WRITE THAT PROGRAM.

I TOOK THE LIBERTY OF UPDATING YOUR RESUME. I'M GUESSING YOU'LL NEED IT SOON.

SOMEDAY WHEN I BECOME THE SUPREME RULER OF EARTH...

I'LL ORDER EVERYBODY TO GO OUTSIDE ONCE A DAY AND RUN AROUND WITH THEIR MOUTHS OPEN.

BECAUSE YOU SUPPORT FRESH AIR AND EXERCISE?

BECAUSE I HATE FLIES.

THANKS FOR MAKING THAT PRODUCT MOCK-UP LAST WEEK. THE CUSTOMER LIKED IT SO MUCH THAT HE ORDERED A THOUSAND!

THAT WAS A **MOCK-UP**! WE DON'T MAKE THAT PRODUCT YET. IT WOULD TAKE THREE YEARS TO MAKE ONE.

JUST GIVE ME A THOUSAND MOCK-UPS. THE FIRST ONE WAS TERRIFIC!

THE MOCK-UP WAS OUR COMPETITOR'S PRODUCT WITH DUCT TAPE OVER THE LOGO.

I'LL NEED YOUR FULL MANAGEMENT SUPPORT IN THIS MEETING WITH SALES.

JUST WATCH THE MASTER AT WORK.

I PROMISED A CUSTOMER A PRODUCT THAT WE DON'T MAKE. YOU NEED TO ENGINEER-UP A THOUSAND UNITS BY EARLY NEXT WEEK.

IS THURSDAY OKAY?

WAIT UNTIL HE FINDS OUT THAT THURSDAY ISN'T "EARLY NEXT WEEK." HEE HEE!

I'M ASSIGNING EACH OF YOU TO A SEPARATE "QUALITY" INITIATIVE.

IS THERE ANY RISK THIS WILL DEVOUR OUR PRODUCTIVE HOURS, LOWER OUR MORALE AND HAVE NO IMPACT ON OUR PROFITABILITY?

AND WE'LL HAVE A CONTEST TO COME UP WITH A NAME FOR THE OVERALL INITIATIVE.

HOW ABOUT "QUALICIDE"?

HE'S WITH THE OTHER MANAGERS IN AN EMPLOYEE RANKING AND RATING SESSION.

YOUR SALARY DEPENDS ON HOW WELL YOUR BOSS CAN DEFEND YOUR PROPOSED RAISE TO THE OTHER MANAGERS.

SOB

I'M FAIRLY SURE THIS DILBERT GUY WORKS FOR YOU.

DOESN'T RING A BELL.

CATBERT, THE EVIL DIRECTOR OF HUMAN RESOURCES

WALLY, IT'S TIME FOR YOUR MANDATORY BLOOD TEST.

I DON'T TAKE DRUGS.

I'M TESTING TO SEE IF YOU'RE STEALING TIME FROM THE COMPANY.

TIME? HOW CAN YOU TEST FOR THAT?

WE TEST YOUR GENERAL HEALTH. IF IT'S GOOD, YOU'RE NOT WORKING ENOUGH HOURS.

YOU THIEF.

CATBERT, THE EVIL DIRECTOR OF HUMAN RESOURCES

ACCORDING TO MY SOURCES, YOU'VE BEEN ENJOYING YOUR JOB, WALLY.

IT WAS TEMPORARY. I DON'T KNOW WHAT GOT INTO ME...

PLEASE REFER TO PAGE ONE OF THE EMPLOYEE MANUAL.

"JOB SATISFACTION IS THE SAME AS STEALING FROM THE COMPANY."

I'LL HAVE TO CHARGE YOU FOR ADMISSION UNLESS I START HEARING SOME SHRIEKS OF PAIN.

IN THE YEAR THAT WE'VE DATED, LIZ, YOU'VE OFTEN MENTIONED VARIOUS PROBLEMS IN YOUR LIFE.

I HAVE COMPILED THOSE PROBLEMS INTO A LIST OF REQUIREMENTS AND DEVELOPED A COMPREHENSIVE SET OF SOLUTIONS.

HOW THOUGHTFUL. I DIDN'T EVEN KNOW I WAS BROKEN.

NO, NO, NOT BROKEN... JUST A BIT BUGGY.

UM... WHEN I'VE SHARED MY FEELINGS WITH YOU, I WASN'T HOPING YOU'D DESIGN AN ACTION PLAN TO SOLVE ALL OF MY PROBLEMS.

WHY ELSE WOULD YOU TELL ME ALL OF YOUR PROBLEMS... UNLESS IT'S SOME DEMENTED PLOT TO MAKE YOURSELF FEEL BETTER AT MY EXPENSE?

YOU WERE RIGHT. IT WAS ALL A DEMENTED PLOT.

I'M TRYING TO GRADUALLY LIFT YOUR VEIL OF IGNORANCE.

OUR NEW "RECOGNITION PROGRAM" ASSIGNS THE NAMES OF PRECIOUS GEMS TO YOUR LEVELS OF PERFORMANCE.

THE HIGHEST LEVEL IS DIAMOND. YOU GET A NEW RING AT EACH LEVEL.

ARE YOU SURE TALC IS A PRECIOUS GEM?

I THINK I SAW IT SPARKLE.

AS YOU CAN SEE FROM MY RING, I'M A MEMBER OF THE "TALC CLUB" AT WORK.

WITH HARD WORK AND A BIT OF LUCK I WILL RISE TO THE NEXT LEVEL: SHALE.

I CAN HONESTLY SAY MY RESPECT FOR YOU HAS NEVER BEEN HIGHER.

SOMEDAY, GOD WILLING, I'LL MAKE IT TO ALUMINUM.

IT'S TIME FOR ME TO UPDATE YOUR OBJECTIVES, ALICE.

WE NEED TARGETS THAT CAN ONLY BE ACHIEVED BY AMAZINGLY HARD WORK PLUS THE CONSTANT SUPPORT OF MANAGEMENT.

I'M BUSY, SO YOU'LL HAVE TO WRITE THEM YOURSELF.

WHAT'S WRONG WITH THIS PICTURE?

THE VOTES ARE IN. I'VE BEEN ELECTED TO THE POSITION OF SUPREME RULER OF EARTH.

I WON IN A LANDSLIDE, THANKS TO LOW VOTER TURNOUT AND THE FACT THAT I VOTED FOR MYSELF MANY TIMES.

I HOPE YOU'LL BE A BENEVOLENT RULER.

I THINK I'LL MAKE CANING AN OLYMPIC EVENT.

MY DOMINION OVER THE PLANET IS NOT WIDELY RECOGNIZED BY THE DOLTS WHO ARE BREATHING MY AIR.

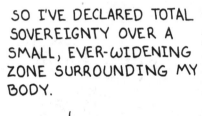

SO I'VE DECLARED TOTAL SOVEREIGNTY OVER A SMALL, EVER-WIDENING ZONE SURROUNDING MY BODY.

HOW BIG IS THE ZONE?

YOU HAVE JUST ENTERED DOGBERT-LAND. PLEASE SHOW YOUR PASSPORT AND LEAVE THE OXYGEN ALONE!

IF WE ARE TO SUCCEED, YOU MUST BECOME CHANGE MASTERS IN AN EVER-CHANGING, CHANGE-ADAPTIVE ENVIRONMENT.

LET ME GET THIS STRAIGHT... EVERY CHANGE SEEMS TO INCREASE OUR WORKLOAD WHILE DECREASING OUR JOB SECURITY AND REAL EARNINGS AFTER INFLATION...

AND THE PROBLEM IS OUR LACK OF FLEXIBILITY?

NOT ENTIRELY. THERE'S ALSO YOUR BAD MORALE.

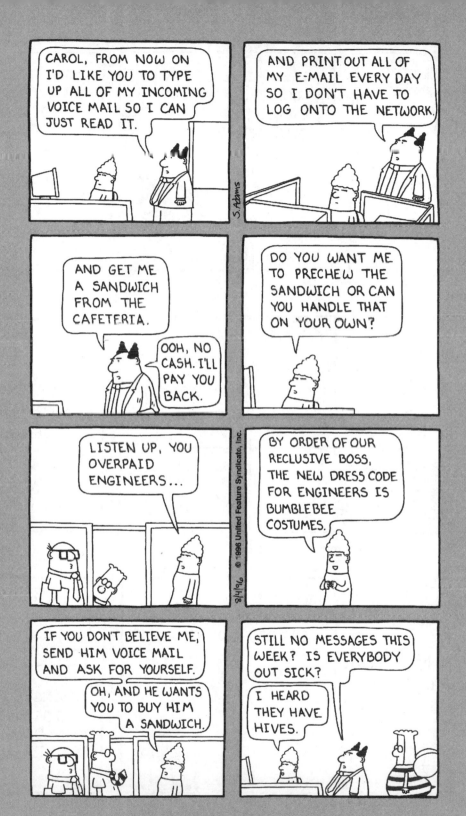

Panel 1: IT'S TIME TO DO PEER-PERFORMANCE REVIEWS!

Panel 2: REMEMBER, THERE'S A LIMITED BUDGET FOR RAISES. YOUR BEST STRATEGY IS TO SLANDER YOUR CO-WORKERS SO THERE'S MORE MONEY FOR YOU!

Panel 3: I PLAN TO SAY VERY NICE THINGS ABOUT YOU.

NICE TRY, WEASEL-BOY.

MANAGING IS EASY WHEN YOU HATE THE EMPLOYEES.

Panel 4: WALLY, THESE PEER REVIEWS ARE LIKE THE FAMOUS "PRISONER'S DILEMMA."

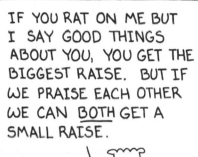

Panel 5: IF YOU RAT ON ME BUT I SAY GOOD THINGS ABOUT YOU, YOU GET THE BIGGEST RAISE. BUT IF WE PRAISE EACH OTHER WE CAN <u>BOTH</u> GET A SMALL RAISE.

Panel 6: WALLY, IF YOU RAT HIM OUT, I'LL LET YOU LOOK AT MY "VICTORIA'S SECRET" CATALOG.

THIS IS EXACTLY WHY THERE ARE NO COED PRISONS.

Panel 7: YOU EMPLOYEES ARE THE KEY TO OUR ECONOMIC SUCCESS.

Panel 8: ANYTIME WE NEED A LITTLE STOCK-PRICE BOOST, WE JUST FIRE ANOTHER BATCH OF YOU. IT'S LIKE PRINTING MONEY!

Panel 9: IN FACT, "INCOMPETENCE" HAS BECOME OUR MOST PROFITABLE PRODUCT.

WOW. IT BEAT OUT "LYING TO CUSTOMERS."

CATBERT: EVIL HR DIRECTOR

HEY, WALLY... BIG LAYOFFS COMING.

I'VE SEEN THE LIST. I KNOW MORE ABOUT YOUR FUTURE THAN YOU DO. BUT IT'S A SECRET.

SADLY, CATS DON'T KEEP SECRETS VERY WELL.

NICE CHAIR.

WE DON'T DO "LAYOFFS" AT THIS COMPANY. BUT YOU HAVE BEEN SELECTED TO PARTICIPATE IN OUR MOBILITY POOL!

AS THE NAME IMPLIES, YOU GET TO SCURRY AROUND TRYING TO FIND A NONEXISTENT INTERNAL JOB BEFORE THE AX FALLS.

HOW'S THIS DIFFERENT FROM A LAYOFF?

WITH LAYOFFS YOU GET TO KEEP YOUR DIGNITY.

I HEAR YOU'RE ON THE LAYOFF LIST, WALLY. HAS ANYONE CLAIMED YOUR CHAIR, YET?

I CLAIMED IT A FEW MINUTES AGO.

LIAR!

OW!

POW!!

I GUESS IT'S TRUE WHAT THEY SAY ABOUT LAYOFFS BEING HARD ON THE SURVIVORS.

DOGBERT: CAREER COUNSELOR

I WAS FIRED ONCE, BUT I CAME BACK AS A CONTRACT EMPLOYEE. LATER I WAS REHIRED AT A HIGHER SALARY.

NOW I'M BEING DOWN-SIZED AGAIN. DO YOU THINK THEY'LL BE DUMB ENOUGH TO HIRE ME A THIRD TIME?

YOUR STORY REMINDS ME OF THE PARABLE OF THE ANT AND THE SPIDER.

REALLY? HOW?

THEY'RE BOTH BORING.

DOGBERT: CAREER COUNSELOR

THE COMPANY WON'T LAY YOU OFF IF ENOUGH PEOPLE QUIT FIRST.

YOUR BEST STRATEGY IS TO CONVINCE YOUR CO-WORKERS THAT THEIR JOBS ARE INTOLERABLE.

WE DO THIS FOR ALL THE YOUNG EMPLOYEES, ASOK. I'LL CAPTURE ON VIDEO THE EXACT MOMENT THAT YOUR LIFE FORCE LEAVES YOUR BODY.

GOOD NEWS, WALLY. MOST OF OUR SMART EMPLOYEES QUIT TO GET MUCH BETTER JOBS ELSEWHERE. NOW WE DON'T HAVE TO DO ANY DOWNSIZING.

YOUR JOB IS SAFE. WE NEED YOU TO DO THE WORK OF ALL THE PEOPLE WHO LEFT.

IS IT JUST ME... OR IS THE QUALITY OF "GOOD NEWS" REALLY GOING DOWNHILL LATELY?

I'D HAVE TO SAY YOU'RE BOTH GOING DOWNHILL.

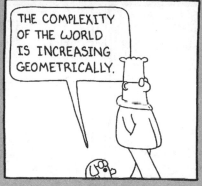

I AM ONLY A LOWLY INTERN, BUT I SEE AN OBVIOUS SOLUTION TO YOUR PROBLEM.

JUST CLICK HERE... CLEAR YOUR BUFFERS AND INITIALIZE THE LINK... NOW USE THIS CODE PATCH FOR THE MEMORY LEAK.

THIS IS FUNNY IF YOU CONSIDER THAT YOUR SALARY IS TWICE AS MUCH AS MINE.

I'M LAUGHING ON THE INSIDE.

ASOK THE INTERN

I CAME IN OVER THE WEEKEND AND LOOKED AT THE DESIGN YOU'VE BEEN WORKING WITH ALL YEAR.

IT TURNS OUT THAT YOU COULD HAVE BUILT THE UNIT AT HALF THE COST WITH JUST ONE MINOR CHANGE.

IS IT TRUE I CAN WIN AWARDS FOR THIS SORT OF THING?

FETCH THE INTERNAPULT.

I'M GOING TO USE BAD GRAMMAR MORE OFTEN.

MY LEADERSHIP WILL CHANGE THE LANGUAGE THROUGH THE PRINCIPLE OF COMMON USAGE.

AND I WON'T STOP UNTIL THE ENTIRE LANGUAGE IS REDUCED TO GRUNTING AND POINTING! BUWAHA-HA HA!!

I REALLY GOT RIPPED OFF BY THAT DOG OBEDIENCE SCHOOL.

CATBERT THE HR DIRECTOR

MORALE IS LOW BECAUSE THE EMPLOYEES ARE UNDERPAID.

YOU CAN COMPENSATE BY HAVING MORE FREQUENT PERFORMANCE REVIEWS. THEY LOVE FEEDBACK.

THE HARDEST PART IS KEEPING A STRAIGHT FACE.

TELL ME AGAIN WHY I'D WANT MORALE TO BE HIGH?

GOOD NEWS, ALICE. I'M GOING TO HAVE QUARTERLY PERFORMANCE REVIEWS TO BOOST MORALE.

WOW! IN ADDITION TO WORKING SIXTEEN HOURS A DAY IN THIS BIG BOX, NOW I'LL GET 300% MORE CRITICISM!

I'LL HAVE A CHANCE TO HEAR EMPLOYEE CONCERNS FOUR TIMES A YEAR.

I ASSUME COMPRE-HENSION WILL REMAIN ON THE BICEN-TENNIAL PLAN.

AT FIRST I THOUGHT YOU COMMITTED ME TO AN IMPOSSIBLE DEADLINE. BUT I HAVE A THEORETICAL SOLUTION.

IT INVOLVES FLYING AROUND THE EARTH SO FAST THAT I TRAVEL BACK TO THE PAST.

AND THEN YOU'LL HAVE ENOUGH TIME?

NO, THEN I'LL GIVE YOUR PARENTS THIS PAMPHLET ON CONTRACEPTION.

STILL
PUMPED
FROM USING THE
MOUSE

A DILBERT® Book by Scott Adams

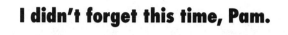

I didn't forget this time, Pam.

Introduction

In the past few years several great cartoonists have decided to retire, much to the sadness of their fans. It makes me feel like the guy who took the home movies of the Kennedy assassination—the right side of my brain is saying, "What a horrible tragedy," while the left side is making those little cash register noises.

When the announcement of Bill Watterson's retirement came out several reporters called me to get my reaction. The phone conversations went like this:

Reporter: "What do you think about Watterson retiring?"

Me: "Hee hee. Oops."

Reporter: "Are you giggling?"

Me: "Um, no, I'm weeping over the loss of an excellent comic strip."

Reporter: "What's that music in the background?"

Me: "My cats are forming a conga line. They don't seem to appreciate the sadness of this situation."

Cats: "Tequila!!!!"

Maybe it didn't go exactly like that, but you get the general picture.

Anyway, the question I'm most often asked lately is whether I'm also "burned out" and planning to retire. The answer is no, I haven't made enough money to be "burned out" yet. I only have enough money to feel "tired" or maybe "overworked." And frankly, I blame you readers for that.

In any event, quitting just isn't my style. I'm more likely to hire illegal immigrants to do the writing and drawing for me. They might not bring the same wit and artistic integrity to the strip that I do … and it might not be in English … but let's face it, my work isn't a home run every single day either. It'll probably take a decade for anybody to notice. And by then maybe I'll be "burned out" too.

Speaking of home runs, you can still join Dogbert's New Ruling Class (DNRC) before Dogbert conquers the world and makes everybody else our domestic servants. As you might have noticed, the members of the DNRC are brighter and more attractive than the "induhviduals" who have not joined, so don't be an induhvidual.

To join the DNRC, simply put your name on the list for the free Dilbert Newsletter, published approximately "whenever I feel like it," or about four times a year.

If you want to receive the DNRC Newsletter via e-mail, send your e-mail address to:

ScottAdams@aol.com

If you prefer hard copies of the DNRC Newsletter, via snail mail, send your address to:

Dilbert Mailing List
c/o United Media
200 Madison Avenue
New York, NY 10016

S. Adams

http://www.unitedmedia.com/comics/dilbert/

DILBERT, YOU'RE BEING TEMPORARILY TRANSFERRED TO THE FIELD SALES ORGANIZATION.

NORMALLY WE USE THESE ASSIGNMENTS TO ROUND SOMEBODY OUT FOR MANAGEMENT. BUT IN THIS CASE I'M JUST YANKING YOUR CHAIN!

12-14

YOU'RE OVER-COMMUNICATING AGAIN, SIR.

PLUS, I HATE THE MANAGER OF SALES.

SO... DILBERT, WELCOME TO THE SALES DEPARTMENT. I'M TINA, YOUR NEW BOSS.

HI

AS THE NEW GUY, YOU GET THE CUSTOMERS WHO DESPISE OUR PRODUCTS AND WANT TO HURT US PERSONALLY.

12-15

I HATE YOU! I HATE YOU!

YOU'LL BE SELLING TO THE SMALL BUSINESS MARKET. HE'S YOUR BEST ACCOUNT.

WELCOME TO SALES TRAINING.

12-16

AS YOU KNOW, OUR COMPANY MAKES OVER-PRICED, INFERIOR PRODUCTS. WE TRY TO COMPENSATE BY SETTING HIGH SALES QUOTAS.

WE DON'T <u>ASK</u> YOU TO ACT ILLEGALLY, BUT IT'S PRETTY MUCH THE ONLY WAY TO REACH QUOTA. OKAY, THAT'S IT FOR TRAINING. ANY QUESTIONS?

DILBERT THE SALESMAN...

YOUR COMPETITOR WAS HERE AN HOUR AGO...

HE PROMISED ME A MASSAGE FROM HELGA IF I BUY FROM HIS COMPANY. WHAT'S YOUR OFFER?

I'LL GIVE YOU MY HOUSE FOR HELGA.

YOU'RE NEW AT THIS...

YOU'VE NEVER ACCEPTED ME IN YOUR FAMILY BECAUSE I'M A LITTLE RAT.

BUT I'LL BE TESTING A DRUG AT THE LAB THAT WILL CHANGE THAT. NO MORE LITTLE RAT.

YOU WON'T BE A RAT?

DON'T TELL ME IT'S THE "RAT" PART THAT BOTHERS YOU...

I'M TESTING A GROWTH FORMULA AT THE LAB.

I'M SO HAPPY. I'VE OFTEN THOUGHT THAT THE ONLY THING BETTER THAN A RAT IN THE HOUSE IS A <u>GIANT</u> RAT IN THE HOUSE.

YESTERDAY I WOULD HAVE BEEN MIFFED AT YOUR SARCASM. BUT THAT WOULDN'T BE "BIG" OF ME.

BETTER YET, A GIANT, <u>WITTY</u> RAT.

GOOD REPORT, BUT CHANGE THE WORD "USE" TO "UTILIZE" IN EACH CASE.

CHANGE "HELP" TO "FACILITATE" AND REPLACE "DO" WITH "IMPLEMENTATION PHASE."

HMM... IT'S STILL A BIT TOO READABLE.

I COULD REDUCE THE TYPE SIZE AND RUN IT THROUGH THE FAX.

NORMALLY I'M ALL STRESSED OUT DURING THE HOLIDAYS, BUT NOT THIS YEAR.

I ELIMINATED MY SHOPPING STRESS BY GETTING EVERYBODY THE "FLABMASTER THIGH-TONING SUPPORT SOCKS."

THEIR COMMERCIALS SOUND BETTER THE CLOSER YOU GET TO CHRISTMAS.

YOU CAN BUILD MUSCLE JUST LYING ON THE COUCH!

I'M COLLECTING MONEY FOR A GIFT TO A POOR FAMILY THIS CHRISTMAS.

WHAT ARE YOU BUYING FOR THEM?

A CD PLAYER.

THANK YOU FOR MAKING THIS THE MOST SHALLOW GESTURE OF MY LIFE.

I'LL ADD YOUR NAME TO THE CARD.

LET'S SEE... I'VE GOT MY CELLULAR PHONE, MY PAGER, PALM COMPUTER, PERSONAL ORGANIZER, WIRELESS MODEM...

YEAH, I'D SAY I'M PRETTY MUCH THE ENVY OF ENGINEERS EVERYWHERE... LOOKING GOOD... LOOKING GOOD...

WORDS ESCAPE ME...

HERE, I'LL FIRE UP THE OLD THESAURUS.

WALLY, I NOTICE THAT ALL YOU HAVE IS A PAGER AND A CALCULATOR WATCH.

UH-OH

THAT'S PATHETIC COMPARED TO MY VAST ARRAY OF PERSONAL ELECTRONICS. DO YOU YIELD TO MY TECHNICAL SUPERIORITY?

WHEN A MALE ENGINEER CHALLENGES ANOTHER FOR DOMINANCE OF THE PACK, THERE IS A BRIEF RITUAL-ISTIC BATTLE RARELY SEEN BY OUTSIDERS.

STAY BACK, I'VE GOT A COMPASS!!

WIRELESS FAX!

AAGH!

MY VAST ARRAY OF PERSONAL TECHNOLOGY MAKES ME DOMINANT OVER THE LESS-EQUIPPED ENGINEERS.

I AM SUPERIOR TO THEM ALL... WITH THE POSSIBLE EXCEPTION OF...

TECHNO-BILL !!

LOOKS LIKE SOMEBODY JUST HAD A FAX.

269

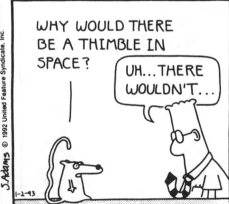

EVERYBODY TAKE ONE AND FASTEN IT SECURELY AROUND YOUR HEAD.

FROM TIME TO TIME I'LL USE MY "BELT-O-AUTHORITY" TO SEND YOU PAINFUL ELECTRIC SHOCKS.

1-4-93

WHEN OUR PERFORMANCE IS BAD?

THAT'S ONE THEORY, SURE.

I'VE HAD ENOUGH OF THOSE WIMPY MANAGEMENT TECHNIQUES LIKE "EMPOWERMENT" AND "QUALITY."

1-5-93

WRITE A BETTER MEMO OR I'LL SEND A STRONG SHOCK TO YOUR HEAD.

THE BEST PART IS THAT IT'S ALL SUBJECTIVE.

THE BOSS IS MAKING US WEAR THESE THINGS ON OUR HEADS SO HE CAN GIVE US PAINFUL SHOCKS WHENEVER HE WANTS.

1-6-93

I'M REWIRING MINE SO IT REDIRECTS THE SIGNAL TO WALLY.

I'M SURE HE'LL SEE THE HUMOR IN THAT.

OKAY, WISEGUY, DO YOU WANT MORE OF THIS?!

MAYBE ONE MORE.

272

I'M GOING TO OPEN A SCHOOL FOR PEOPLE WHO ARE TECHNOLOGY IMBECILES.

I'LL TEACH PEOPLE HOW TO USE AUTOMATIC BANK MACHINES, MICROWAVE OVENS, VIDEO RECORDERS, CD PLAYERS, THAT SORT OF THING...

I THOUGHT HE WAS REASONABLY BRIGHT UNTIL WE GOT THE VCR...

THEY CAN FOOL YOU.

Imbecile Admissions

WELCOME TO DOGBERT'S SCHOOL FOR TECHNOLOGY IMBECILES.

YOU ARE ALL EASILY BAFFLED BY SIMPLE TECHNOLOGY, EVEN THOUGH YOU HAVE NORMAL INTELLIGENCE OTHERWISE.

OF COURSE, I'M GENERALIZING ON THAT LAST POINT.

DEER

DOGBERT'S SCHOOL FOR TECHNOLOGY IMBECILES

CAN ANYBODY SHOW ME WHAT YOU DO WITH A MICROWAVE?

I INSERT THE VIDEO TAPE... THEN I SET THE TIMER FOR NINETY MINUTES...

DOES ANYBODY KNOW WHY IT ISN'T WORKING?

THE FOOL! IT'S BETA!

273

I'M JOINING THE S.E.W.L.T.U.I.F.E.

TO THE LAY DOG, IT'S KNOWN AS THE "SOCIETY OF ENGINEERS WHO LIKE TO USE INITIALS FOR EVERYTHING."

WE USE ACRONYMS TO SET US APART FROM THE UNWASHED MASSES WHO DON'T UNDERSTAND TECHNOLOGY.

B.F.D.*

*BIG FURRY DEAL

...SO, EITHER AN IBM 586 WITH 10 MEG RAM OR MAYBE A SPARC CPU ON A LAN...

...BUT WITH AI AND AVR COMBINED WITH BISDN, WELL, IT'S VERY G.

G?

GOOD.

WHAT ARE YOU DOING?

I'M WRITING AN INSTRUCTION BOOK FOR NEW-BORN BABIES.

YOU DON'T KNOW ANY-THING ABOUT BABIES.

OKAY, I'M NOT AN EXPERT, BUT COMPARED TO THE PEOPLE WHO HAVE BABIES...

WHICH END DO I PUT THE CHEESE STEAK IN?

"ALTHOUGH RAISING CHILDREN IS DIFFICULT, BE ASSURED THAT YOU WILL GET HELP FROM A POWER GREATER THAN YOURSELF."

"TEACH YOUR CHILDREN ABOUT THE HIGHER POWER AND ABOUT THE 'GREAT BOOK' WHICH WILL GIVE THEM DIRECTION."

THEY'RE CALLED "TV LISTINGS." WITHOUT THEM, YOU'RE JUST FLIPPING.

THERE'S DILBERT... I'LL SNEAK UP AND HUG HIS LEG UNTIL HE LOVES ME AND ACCEPTS ME IN THE FAMILY.

© 1993 United Feature Syndicate, Inc.

A RAT IS CLINGING TO MY LEG.

I HAD THAT PROBLEM TILL I SWITCHED TO "OLD SPICE."

MY NEW STYLE OF MANAGEMENT IS EXHAUSTING ME.

I HEARD SOME PEOPLE TALKING ABOUT "MBWA" OR "MANAGEMENT BY WALKING AROUND."

I WALKED ALL THE WAY TO THE PARK AND BACK. BUT I CAN'T SAY THAT I SEE MUCH IMPROVEMENT AROUND HERE.

277

I'M FEELING ILL. I THINK I'LL STAY HOME TODAY.

GREAT... NOW YOU'LL TRY TO MAKE ME FEEL SORRY FOR YOU SO I'LL WAIT ON YOU ALL DAY WELL, THAT'S A LOUSY THING TO DO TO A FRIEND.

GEE, I'M SORRY. CAN I GET YOU ANYTHING WHILE I'M UP?

TEA WITH LEMON. AND SOME WAFFLES.

TO PROTECT OUR ENVIRONMENT, I'VE ORDERED THAT INK BE REMOVED FROM ALL COPIERS, PRINTERS AND PENS.

RESEARCH SHOWS THAT MANY SQUIDS CAN BE SPARED BY REDUCING OUR INK USAGE.

I DON'T THINK WE GET OUR INK FROM SQUIDS, SIR.

OH, RIGHT... NEXT YOU'LL SAY WE DON'T GET OUR "ELMER'S" GLUE FROM COWS.

FIRST ON THE AGENDA IS A DISCUSSION OF THE COMPANY'S NEW PAPER RECYCLING PROGRAM.

WE TALKED ABOUT THAT LAST TIME... HEY, THIS IS LAST WEEK'S AGENDA.

YOU SPOTTED THE ONE DRAWBACK.

SOMETIMES I WONDER, HOW WOULD MY LIFE BE DIFFERENT IF ALL WHALES WERE EXTINCT?

IT'S NOT LIKE THEY DO ANYTHING FOR US. YOU NEVER HEAR OF SEEING-EYE WHALES. THEY CAN'T FETCH THE PAPER OR DRAG YOU OUT OF A BURNING BUILDING...

DON'T YOU THINK THE WORLD HAS TOO MANY FAT, WORTHLESS, MAMMALS?

I WAS JUST THINKING THAT, SIR.

1-21

HERE'S MY NEW BUSINESS CARD. I'M A ROMANCE INTERPRETER.

1-22

FOR A SMALL FEE I'LL ACCOMPANY YOU ON DATES AND TRANSLATE BETWEEN MALE AND FEMALE LANGUAGE.

SHE'S TELLING A POINTLESS STORY ABOUT WORK. BY ANNOYING YOU IN THIS WAY SHE HOPES TO FORM A CLOSER BOND.

BLAH BLAH BLAH

DOGBERT IS A ROMANCE INTERPRETER

HE'S TELLING YOU HOW TO LOGICALLY SOLVE ALL OF THE EMOTIONAL PROBLEMS YOU SEEM TO HAVE.

BLAH BLAH BLAH

HE REASONS THAT IF HE CAN FIX YOUR PROBLEMS HE WON'T HAVE TO HEAR ABOUT THEM ANYMORE.

BLAH BLAH BLAH

HE HOPES THAT THE WISDOM AND COMPASSION HE JUST FAKED WAS ENOUGH TO AROUSE YOU. NOW HE WILL TALK ABOUT HIMSELF.

BLAH BLAH ME

THE COMPANY IS A BILLION DOLLARS BELOW ITS EARNINGS PROJECTIONS.

FROM NOW ON, ONLY THE MANAGERS AT MY LEVEL OR ABOVE MAY EAT DONUTS AT COMPANY MEETINGS.

THIS WON'T BE EASY FOR ANY OF US. HECK, I DON'T EVEN KNOW IF I CAN EAT THIS MANY DONUTS.

THEIR CARS ARE ALWAYS CLEAN

THEY WRITE LETTERS TO EXPRESS THEIR OUTRAGE

Dear Editor,
The funny pages is no place for sarcasm! Think about the children !

THEY READ THE SAME BOOK MORE THAN ONCE.

THEY ARE THE PEOPLE WITH WAY TOO MUCH TIME ON THEIR HANDS.

HEE HEE

HI, GUYS. I'M WENDELL J. STONE THE FOURTH, RECENT STANFORD MBA AND BRAND NEW TO THE WORKFORCE.

LOOK, "WEN-DULL," WE AREN'T IMPRESSED BY YOUR EDUCATION. AT THIS COMPANY IT'S THE QUALITY OF YOUR WORK THAT COUNTS!

I'M YOUR NEW SENIOR VICE PRESIDENT, AND I WANT YOU TO LICK THE TAR OFF MY PORSCHE NOW.

OKAY, BUT WATCH THE QUALITY OF MY WORK!

287

DOGBERT IS A CREATIVITY CONSULTANT

WE DON'T NEED ANY OF YOUR "INTUITION" MUMBO JUMBO. WE NEED QUANTITATIVE DATA!

THE ONLY WAY TO MAKE DECISIONS IS TO PULL NUMBERS OUT OF THE AIR, CALL THEM "ASSUMPTIONS," AND CALCULATE THE NET PRESENT VALUE.

OF COURSE, YOU HAVE TO USE THE RIGHT DISCOUNT RATE, OTHERWISE IT'S MEANINGLESS.

GO AWAY.

DOGBERT IS A CREATIVITY CONSULTANT

HERE'S MY FINAL REPORT ON YOUR COMPANY.

I'VE CONCLUDED THAT YOU'RE DOOMED. YOU WASTE TOO MUCH MONEY ON CONSULTANTS.

YOU'RE A CONSULTANT.

IRONIC, ISN'T IT?

THIS IS IT... THE CRITICAL THIRD DATE.

THIS IS WHEN THEY CASUALLY MENTION ANY HIDDEN DEFORMITIES OR HORRIBLE SECRETS TO SEE IF YOU STILL LIKE THEM.

SOME PEOPLE SAY YOU SHOULD STOP DATING AFTER YOU MARRY A MOB BOSS.

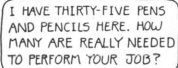

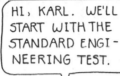

IN ORDER TO BUILD TEAM SPIRIT I'VE DECIDED YOU SHOULD HAVE LUNCH TOGETHER ONCE A WEEK.

I WON'T BE THERE MYSELF BECAUSE IT WOULD SERIOUSLY CUT INTO MY FREE TIME.

BESIDES, IT'S MY JOB TO MOTIVATE, NOT GET BOGGED DOWN IN THE DETAILS.

WHAT ARE YOU UP TO, TED?

I'M WORKING LIKE A DOG LATELY.

I'D BETTER NOT ASK.

SCRATCH SCRATCH

I FOUND A TYPO IN THE BUDGET SPREAD-SHEET... IT'S TOO LATE TO FIX IT.

WE TRANSFERRED ONE JOB TO ANOTHER GROUP BUT ACCIDENTALLY KEPT THE MONEY AND HEAD-COUNT.

...SO, WE STILL PAY YOU BUT YOU AREN'T ALLOWED TO DO WORK.

THIS IS THE HAPPIEST DAY OF MY LIFE.

HI, I'M TIM ZUMPH, WRITER OF THE FAMOUS MEMO OF FEBRUARY THIRD, 1978...

I REMEMBER IT SO CLEARLY. MY BOSS WALKED RIGHT UP AND SAID "NICE MEMO, TIM." AND IT WASN'T EVEN TIME FOR MY ANNUAL PERFORMANCE REVIEW.

I STILL KEEP A COPY WITH ME.

TYPO...

FROM NOW ON, YOUR RAISES WILL BE PARTLY DEPENDENT ON AN EVALUATION BY YOUR CO-WORKERS.

HYPOTHETICALLY, IF MY CO-WORKERS GOT SMALL RAISES THEN WOULDN'T THERE BE MORE AVAILABLE IN THE BUDGET FOR ME?

THAT DIDN'T LAST LONG, EVEN BY OUR STANDARDS.

I'VE BEEN SAYING FOR YEARS THAT "EMPLOYEES ARE OUR MOST VALUABLE ASSET."

IT TURNS OUT THAT I WAS WRONG. MONEY IS OUR MOST VALUABLE ASSET. EMPLOYEES ARE NINTH.

I'M AFRAID TO ASK WHAT CAME IN EIGHTH.

CARBON PAPER.

LOOK EVERYONE, I'M ENGAGED!

HEY, IT'S ONE OF THOSE "NEAR DIAMOND" RINGS THEY WERE SELLING ON THE TV SHOPPING CHANNEL FOR $29.95.

© 1993 United Feature Syndicate, Inc.

UH... OF COURSE IT HAS A LIST PRICE OF OVER A HUNDRED DOLLARS...

OOH, GOOD SAVE.

GEE, LINDA, IF YOU DON'T MIND SOME CONSTRUCTIVE CRITICISM, THAT DRESS MAKES YOU LOOK PUDGY.

© 1993 United Feature Syndicate, Inc.

HAAIII!!!

I STILL DON'T UNDERSTAND WOMEN, BUT I THINK WHEN THEY YELL "HAAIII" IT MEANS THEY LIKE THE DRESS THEY'RE WEARING.

I DON'T UNDERSTAND WHY PHOTOGRAPHERS TRY SO HARD TO GET EMBARRASSING PICTURES OF CELEBRITIES.

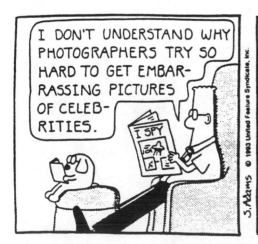

I SPY

© 1993 United Feature Syndicate, Inc.

HECK, I COULD JUST SCAN THE CELEBRITY PHOTOS INTO MY COMPUTER AND CREATE ANY EMBARRASSING SITUATION YOU CAN THINK OF.

I SPY

I THINK CINDY CRAWFORD SHOULD LOOK MORE REPULSED.

THIS IS BEFORE WE KISS.

I JUST READ THAT A NEW COMPUTER CHIP IS ON THE MARKET. YOUR MACHINE IS OUT OF DATE.

YOU'RE BEHIND THE CURVE. TECHNOLOGY IS RACING AHEAD WITHOUT YOU. YOU'RE NO LONGER STATE-OF-THE-ART OR LEADING EDGE.

SOMETIMES PEOPLE LIKE YOU CAN GET JOBS IN MUSEUMS.

I BOUGHT THIS THING YESTERDAY!!

I'M SO MAD... I JUST BOUGHT A NEW COMPUTER AND IT'S ALREADY OBSOLETE.

DON'T FEEL BAD. THE OTHER ENGINEERS WON'T LOOK DOWN ON YOU JUST BECAUSE YOU'RE BEHIND THE TECHNOLOGY CURVE.

YEAH, WE WILL.

NOT RIGHT IN FRONT OF HIM.

LAPTOP COMPUTERS ARE OUTDATED. YOU WANT OUR NEW FINGERNAIL MODELS.

SALE 50¢

NEW ↓

YOU GLUE THEM PERMANENTLY TO EACH NAIL. THEY SENSE WHERE EACH FINGER IS AT ALL TIMES. YOU DON'T NEED A KEYBOARD.

OF COURSE, SOME PEOPLE PREFER THAT THEIR COMPUTER NOT KNOW WHERE THEIR FINGERS ARE AT ALL TIMES.

DAVE, ABOUT LAST NIGHT...

299

DILBERT, I NEED YOU TO STOP EVERYTHING AND DO THIS EMERGENCY BUDGET EXERCISE.

ESTIMATE THE BUDGET IMPACT OF REPLACING ALL THE ENGINEERS WITH DECORATIVE PLANTS.

LATER, I'LL SUMMARIZE EVERYBODY'S INPUTS INTO A BULLET POINT, LIKE "OXYGEN IS GOOD."

WOULD THESE BE RENTED PLANTS?

I SUMMARIZED THE BUDGET IMPACTS ON SIX HUNDRED PROJECTS WITH THOSE THREE BULLET POINTS.

"- OXYGEN IS GOOD
- COMPETITION IS BAD
- I LIKE JELLO"

DO YOU THINK IT'S TOO DETAILED FOR THE SENIOR EXECUTIVES?

TAKE OUT THE "COMPETITION" ONE.

I THINK I'M EVOLVING INTO A FLYING RAT.

I NOTICED THAT MY ARMS ARE FLATTER THAN MY PARENTS' ARMS. IN A MILLION YEARS THIS NATURAL ADVANTAGE WILL BECOME WINGS!

THERE GOES THE HAPPIEST RAT I KNOW.

TOO SOON.

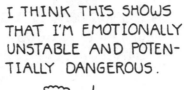

I'M LOOKING FOR A DEVICE THAT WILL ALLOW ME TO TAKE OVER THE SATELLITES OF ALL THE MAJOR BROADCASTERS.

IT WOULD BE ILLEGAL TO SELL SOMETHING LIKE THAT. BUT MAYBE YOU'D BE INTERESTED IN AN ELECTRONIC FISHING LURE INSTEAD.

WINK WINK

FISH CAN'T RESIST THE "HIJACK 3000" LURE. AND IT COMES WITH ITS OWN STUPID-LOOKING HAT!

WINK WINK

CLEVER.

BOB, I NEED YOUR HELP IN MY QUEST TO CONQUER EARTH.

WHAT DO I DO?

I'LL USE MY POWERS OF HYPNOSIS TO CONTROL EVERYBODY WHO SEES ME ON TELEVISION. YOU MUST WHACK EVERYBODY ELSE WITH YOUR MIGHTY TAIL.

DID I EVER MENTION THAT I HAVE SENSITIVE SKIN?

START WITH ACCOUNTANTS. THEY'RE SOFT AND YOU CAN BUILD CALLUSES.

THIS IS DOGBERT... YOU ARE ALL UNDER MY HYPNOTIC POWERS...

I AM THE SUPREME RULER OF EARTH. YOU MUST ALL CARRY DOGBERT POSTERS AND CHANT "DOGBERT IS MY KING."

THAT IS ALL FOR NOW. IF I THINK OF ANYTHING ELSE IMPORTANT I'LL LET YOU KNOW.

...IS MY KING

308

IF I DON'T GET SOME LOVE AND SUPPORT AROUND HERE, I MIGHT TURN TO A LIFE OF HEINOUS CRIME...

OR WORSE, I COULD BECOME A CERTIFIED PUBLIC ACCOUNTANT...

STOP IT. YOU'RE SCARING ME...

I'M GOOD WITH NUMBERS.

I HAVE TO GIVE A SPEECH TO THE "SOCIETY OF ENGINEERS" TODAY... I'M A BIT NERVOUS.

SOMETIMES YOU CAN RELAX BY IMAGINING THE AUDIENCE IS NAKED.

WHOA! CANCEL THAT. I JUST PICTURED FOUR HUNDRED NAKED ENGINEERS.

TOO LATE.

... AS YOU APPROACHED THE SPEED OF LIGHT YOU WOULD BECOME INFINITELY DENSE.

THEN WOULD YOU BE FORCED TO TAKE A JOB AS A HIGH SCHOOL GYM TEACHER?

THE BOOK CHANGES SUBJECTS AT THIS POINT.

SOUNDS LIKE A COVER-UP.

A SMALL BAND OF THE CREATURES WERE KNOWN TO LIVE HIGH IN AN ARTIFICIAL STRUCTURE.

ON MY WAY TO STUDY THEM I TOOK NOTE OF THE NATIVE VEGETATION.

RENTED

THE YOUNGER MALES WERE AT PLAY. THEY BECAME SELF-CONSCIOUS WHEN WATCHED.

THE DOMINANT MALE HAD A GRAY BACK. HE CONTROLLED THE OTHERS BY WAVING LITTLE ENVELOPES.

THERE WERE FEW FEMALES IN THE GROUP. THE LESS DOMINANT MALES HAD NO CHANCE OF MATING.

UNLIKE OTHER SPECIES THEY HAD NO INSTINCT FOR GROOMING.

WANT TO GROOM?

DROP DEAD.

4-11

MY TIME WAS UP. BUT I WILL MISS THEM, THOSE...

ENGINEERS IN THE MIST

HOW LONG ARE YOU SUPPOSED TO MICROWAVE POPCORN?

DON'T GET TOO CLOSE-- I FOUND OUT THAT MY BALDNESS IS CAUSED BY TOO MUCH TESTOSTERONE.

NOW WITH MY HAIR GONE I'M AFRAID THE TESTOSTERONE WILL START FLINGING OUT OF MY PORES.

HEY! YOU GOT SOME ON MY SHIRT!

DO YOU HAVE A PROBLEM WITH THAT?

BEING BALD ISN'T SO BAD. WITH ALL THIS TESTOSTERONE, MEN WILL FEAR ME AND WOMEN WILL DESIRE ME.

TAKE A HIKE, FUZZY. SHE'S MINE NOW.

I DO FIND YOU STRANGELY ATTRACTIVE.

TESTOSTERONE; YOU'RE HELPLESS.

GEE, WALLY, YOU SURE HAVE BEEN POPULAR WITH WOMEN SINCE THE TESTOSTERONE STARTED SPEWING FROM YOUR HEAD.

IT'S AMAZING... I EVEN BOUGHT A PICKUP TRUCK AND A RIFLE SO I CAN HUNT AFTER WORK.

WHAT DO YOU HUNT AROUND HERE?

PIGEONS ARE THE MOST CONVENIENT... DON'T EVEN HAVE TO GET OUT OF THE TRUCK.

MAYBE IT'S BECAUSE OF MY HIGH TESTOSTERONE LEVELS, BUT I COULDN'T RESIST GETTING MY PICKUP JACKED UP.

I THOUGHT IT WOULD BE MORE FRIGHTENING TO THE PEOPLE I TAILGATE.

THE ONLY PROBLEM IS THAT YOU CAN'T LET PEOPLE SEE YOU TRYING TO GET IN IT.

LIFE HAS BEEN GREAT SINCE THE TESTOSTERONE STARTED SPEWING FROM MY HEAD.

IT LOOKS LIKE THE FLOW IS STOPPING.

WAIT-A-MINUTE. WHY WAS I TOUCHING YOU?

I HOPE YOU WON'T BE SHALLOW ABOUT THIS.

...AND PEOPLE WHO DON'T BOTHER TO VOTE HAVE NO RIGHT TO COMPLAIN.

WHY NOT?

WHY NOT? IT'S OBVIOUS. NO VOTE MEANS NO RIGHT TO COMPLAIN. YOU CAN'T GET MUCH MORE LOGICAL THAN THAT.

BESIDES, THAT'S HOW I WAS RAISED.

YOU WERE RAISED BY BUMPER STICKERS?

315

THE LOCAL SCHOOL WANTS SOMEBODY TO TALK TO THE KIDS ABOUT A CAREER AS AN ENGINEER.

I'M GIVING THIS PLUM ASSIGNMENT TO YOU BECAUSE YOU'RE SUCH A GOOD ROLE MODEL.

HEE HEE

IT'S MORE SINCERE SOUNDING WHEN YOU DON'T GIGGLE.

REMEMBER, CHILDREN ARE OUR FUTURE!

DILBERT HAS AGREED TO TALK TO THE CLASS ABOUT EXCITING CAREERS IN THE FIELD OF ENGINEERING!

THERE'S MORE TO BEING AN ENGINEER THAN JUST WRITING TECHNICAL MEMOS THAT NOBODY READS.

ONCE IN A WHILE, SOMEBODY READS ONE. THEN YOU HAVE TO FIND A SCAPEGOAT, OR USE SOME VACATION TIME AND HOPE IT ALL BLOWS OVER.

DILBERT TALKS TO A CLASS ABOUT CAREER OPTIONS.

ENGINEERING IS ONE OF THE BEST CAREERS AVAILABLE.

FOR THE NEXT TWENTY YEARS I'LL SIT IN A BIG BOX CALLED A CUBICLE. IT'S LIKE A RESTROOM STALL BUT WITH LOWER WALLS.

I SPEND MOST OF MY TIME HOPING THE ELECTROMAGNETIC FIELDS FROM MY OFFICE EQUIPMENT AREN'T KILLING ME.

DILBERT TALKS TO A CLASS ABOUT CAREER OPTIONS.

AND DON'T FORGET THE SOCIAL LIFE THAT COMES WITH BEING AN ENGINEER.

NINETY PERCENT OF ALL ENGINEERS ARE GUYS, SO IT'S A BONANZA OF DATING OPPORTUNITIES FOR THE LADIES WHO ENTER THE FIELD.

FOR THE MEN, THERE ARE THESE LITTLE VIDEO GAME DEVICES...

BEEP BEEP

WOULD I BE ALLOWED TO DATE A NON-ENGINEER?

DILBERT TALKS TO A CLASS ABOUT CAREER OPTIONS.

THE GOAL OF EVERY ENGINEER IS TO RETIRE WITHOUT GETTING BLAMED FOR A MAJOR CATASTROPHE.

ENGINEERS PREFER TO WORK AS "CONSULTANTS" ON PROJECT TEAMS. THAT WAY THERE'S NO REAL WORK, BLAME IS SPREAD ACROSS THE GROUP, AND YOU CAN CRUSH ANY IDEA FROM MARKETING!

...AND SOMETIMES YOU GET FREE DONUTS JUST FOR SHOWING UP!

GET OUT OF MY CLASS-ROOM.

LOOK WHAT I GOT FOR MY COMPUTER! IT'S A ROMOSTATIC REAL-TIME DATA COMPRESSION PROCESSOR!

OOOH... I CAN'T WAIT TO PLUG YOU IN, MY LITTLE DARLING. I'VE WAITED SO LONG.

OH YES! YES!

DOES THE CHURCH KNOW ABOUT THIS?

319

I'M GOING TO START-UP A TELEVISION NEWS NETWORK THAT ONLY REPORTS HAPPY STORIES.

IN SPORTS, FIFTY PERCENT OF THE TEAMS WON THEIR GAMES YESTERDAY. AND ALL THE PLAYERS ARE MILLIONAIRES — MOST OF WHOM HAVE NO SERIOUS DRUG PROBLEMS.

OUR PERSON OF THE WEEK IS DARRYL, WHO, DESPITE HIS TINY BRAIN, FOUND SUCCESS THROUGH A LIFE OF CRIME.
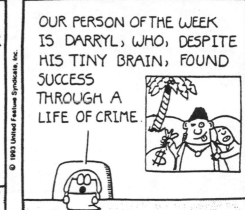

DOGBERT'S GOOD NEWS SHOW

NINE OUT OF TEN PEOPLE HAVE JOBS... THREE BILLION PEOPLE HAD A NICE DAY TODAY... AND THE FOREST HAS PLENTY OF OWLS.

REGULAR NEWS SHOW

A HUGE ASTEROID COULD DESTROY EARTH! AND BY COINCIDENCE, THAT'S THE SUBJECT OF TONIGHT'S MINISERIES.

WE'LL ALL DIE!!

BACK TO DOGBERT...

IN SCIENCE, RESEARCHERS PROVED THAT THIS SIMPLE DEVICE CAN KEEP IDIOTS OFF OF YOUR TELEVISION SCREEN.

CLICK

...THEN I SAID "WHAT ABOUT AN OPTICAL DISK FILE SERVER."

SO BORING, FALLING ASLEEP...

WHUMP

I DON'T KNOW HOW SHE DIED. I WAS TELLING HER ABOUT AN OPTICAL...

ZZZZZZ

325

DILBERT, I WANT YOU TO HELP SUSAN PUT THE DEPARTMENT BUDGET TOGETHER.

BUDGET?!

NO, PLEASE! I'LL BE BRANDED FOR LIFE. THE OTHER ENGINEERS WILL SPIT ON ME.

DARN, HIS GUARD IS UP.

I'LL HAVE TO WEAR A RAINCOAT TO WORK!

5-10

DILBERT IS ASSIGNED TO PREPARE THE BUDGET.

YOU'LL HAVE TO LEARN OUR BUDGET SYSTEM.

IT WAS DEVELOPED 400 YEARS AGO BY A CRAZED MONK WHO SEALED HIMSELF IN A WINE CASK.

5-11

UNFORTUNATELY, WE STILL HAVE HIM.

HEY, I'VE GOT ANOTHER IDEA.

THE OTHER ENGINEERS SHUN ME BECAUSE I'M ASSIGNED TO WORK ON THE BUDGET.

SHUN

5-12

THEY KNOW I COULD POUNCE ANY MOMENT AND ASK INANE HYPOTHETICAL BUDGET QUESTIONS.

SHUN

WHAT IF YOU ONLY HAD HALF AS MUCH ELECTRICITY NEXT YEAR?

TOO LATE. I SHUNNED YOU.

HEY, "DIL-BUTT," I HEAR THEY GOT YOU DOING BUDGET WORK NOW.

HA HA! IT MUST BE REALLY EXCITING WORK. I MEAN, GOSH, MAKING ALL THOSE NUMBERS ADD UP.

5-13

HA HA! I'M GLAD I HAVE A REAL JOB!

NOT ANY-MORE.

CLICK

HOW CAN I BE SURE I'M A RAT?

WHAT IF I'M REALLY SOMETHING ELSE — LIKE A POTATO — AND I JUST THINK I'M A RAT?

5-14

I THINK, THEREFORE I'M A YAM.

IT WOULD EXPLAIN A LOT.

I NEVER LEARNED TO READ, BUT IT DIDN'T MATTER BECAUSE I WAS A GREAT ATHLETE.

5-15

THEN CAME THE MULTI-MILLION DOLLAR CONTRACT, WHICH I SPENT ON DRUGS. EVENTUALLY I WAS BANNED FROM SPORTS. I QUIT DRUGS BECAUSE I COULDN'T AFFORD IT.

NOW I'M A MOTIVA-TIONAL SPEAKER.

HAVE YOU MOTI-VATED ANYBODY TO BECOME ILLITERATE YET?

I GAVE FIVE HUNDRED DOLLARS TO CHARITY THIS YEAR.

I BELIEVE IT'S MY MORAL DUTY TO HELP THOSE LESS FORTUNATE.

FIVE HUNDRED DOLLARS?

WHAT KIND OF MORALITY IS THAT?

PEOPLE ARE STARVING AND YOU STILL HAVE PLENTY OF MONEY LEFT FOR YOUR HOBBIES.

ACCORDING TO YOUR MORAL CODE IT'S MORE IMPORTANT FOR YOU TO HAVE A NEW COMPUTER THAN FOR POOR PEOPLE TO EAT.

MORALITY? HA! YOU SPENT FIVE HUNDRED BUCKS TO EASE YOUR OWN GUILT!

AND IT WORKED. I FEEL PRETTY GOOD.

HOW MUCH DID YOU GIVE TO CHARITY?

A THOUSAND. THAT'S WHY I'M SO TORQUED.

329

YOU'RE WONDERING HOW TO HANDLE THE GOOD NIGHT KISS...

UH

BY A VOTE OF TWO TO ZERO WE'VE DECIDED NOT TO KISS YOU. AND DEBBIE HAS THREATENED A FILIBUSTER ON THE HANDSHAKE ISSUE.

IT'S A BLUFF.

NICE WEATHER TODAY. HAVE YOU SEEN ANY GOOD MOVIES? HOW ABOUT THE ECONOMY, HUH?

5-20

COMPANY HEADQUARTERS

DOES ANYBODY HAVE A PLAN FOR GETTING RID OF THE EMPLOYEES?

WELL, THEY'RE BAD AT MATH; WE COULD OFFER DECEPTIVELY SMALL SUMS OF MONEY TO PEOPLE WHO RETIRE.

HEY, THIS COULD BE GOOD.

IT'S BEEN A LONG TIME SINCE I HAD TO CALCULATE THE COSINE OF ANYTHING.

5-21

GOOD REPORT... BUT ADD A SENTENCE THAT SAYS MICRO-ROBOTICS IS A DEAD-END TECHNOLOGY.

BUT THAT'S THE EXACT OPPOSITE OF MY POINT! IF I ADD THAT, THE WHOLE REPORT WOULD BE A CONFUSING AND SENSELESS WASTE OF TIME!

THAT'S OKAY. WE JUST WON'T LET ANYBODY ELSE SEE IT.

IS THIS A WIN-WIN SCENARIO?

5-22

333

335

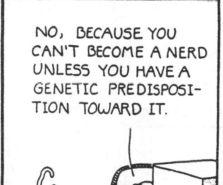

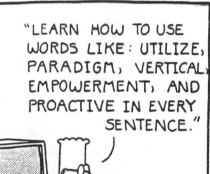

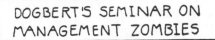

Panel 1:
DOGBERT'S SEMINAR ON MANAGEMENT ZOMBIES

THE SUCCESSFUL ZOMBIE KNOWS HOW TO SQUASH THE CREATIVITY OF CO-WORKERS.

Panel 2:
WHEN YOU HEAR A NEW IDEA, ADOPT A FACIAL EXPRESSION WHICH CONVEYS BOTH FEAR AND AN UTTER LACK OF COMPREHENSION.

Panel 3:
THOSE OF YOU WHO WORK IN MARKETING ONLY NEED TO ADD THE FEAR PART.

WHY IS THAT?

Panel 4:

DOGBERT'S SEMINAR ON MANAGEMENT ZOMBIES

TO BE A ZOMBIE YOU MUST DRINK THE ZOMBIE ELIXIR.

Panel 5:
THE ZOMBIE ELIXIR WILL REMOVE ANY DISTRACTING THOUGHTS OF SLEEP OR FAMILY LIFE.

Panel 6:

IT LOOKS LIKE COFFEE.

YOU HAVE TO ADD ONE SCOOP OF ZOMBIE SUGAR.

Panel 7:
DOGBERT'S SEMINAR ON MANAGEMENT ZOMBIES

AS A ZOMBIE, YOU MUST SPEAK IN EMPTY GENERAL-ITIES.

Panel 8:
YOUR BUSINESS PLAN MIGHT SAY "WE STRIVE TO UTILIZE A VARIETY OF TECHNIQUES TO ACCOMPLISH A BROAD SPECTRUM OF RESULTS TOWARD THE BOTTOM LINE."

Panel 9:
HEY! MY SKIN IS GETTING CLAMMY AND I HAVE THE URGE TO CALL A MEETING!

ME TOO!

GOOD... GOOD...

I'VE SEEN THAT LOOK BEFORE. HE'S IN A VIDEO GAME TRANCE.

HE CAN'T MOVE. I'VE GOT TO DO SOMETHING FAST.

6-21

LASSIE MIGHT HAVE HANDLED THIS DIFFERENTLY.

WHAT ARE THOSE DISHES DOING ON DILBERT'S HEAD?

HE'S IN A VIDEO GAME TRANCE. I'M TESTING MY THEORY THAT HE IS UNAWARE OF HIS ENVIRONMENT AND HAS NO DISCERNABLE MENTAL ACTIVITY.

6-22

POOR GUY.

AS YOU KNOW, ALL PROJECTS ARE ASSIGNED ACRONYMS. UNFORTUNATELY, ALL THE GOOD ONES HAVE BEEN USED.

ANY NEW PROJECT WILL HAVE TO USE AN ACRONYM FROM THIS SHORT LIST OF SOMEWHAT LESS DESIRABLE CHOICES.

6-23

WHAT SHOULD I CALL MY NEW PROJECT?

WELL, YOU COULD USE "PHLEGM" OR "PLACENTA."

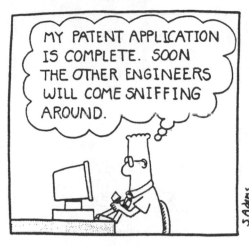

MY PATENT WILL MAKE FIFTY MILLION DOLLARS FOR THE COMPANY, SO I THOUGHT MAYBE YOU COULD AFFORD TO GIVE ME A RAISE.

UNFORTUNATELY, THE PROFIT BUCKET IS NOT CONNECTED TO THE BUDGET BUCKET, SO THERE'S NO MONEY FOR A RAISE.

7-1

I THINK SOME RECOGNITION OF A JOB WELL-DONE IS APPROPRIATE HERE.

THANKS. IT WAS ONE OF MY BETTER EXCUSES.

© 1993 United Feature Syndicate, Inc.

DOGBERT, TELL ME IF YOU THINK MY ILLUSTRATION FOR TOMORROW'S PRESENTATION IS CLEAR.

AH, YES. YOU'RE SAYING THE FACE OF ELVIS WILL APPEAR ON A CREDENZA AFTER BEING STRUCK BY LIGHTNING.

7-2

THAT'S SUPPOSED TO BE A VIDEO TELECONFERENCE.

I DIDN'T KNOW YOU COULD DO THAT WITH A CREDENZA.

© 1993 United Feature Syndicate, Inc.

PLEASE EXCUSE THE ARTWORK IN THIS NEXT DIAGRAM.

WHAT'S THAT? IT LOOKS LIKE ELVIS' FACE ON A CREDENZA! HA HA HA! OR IS IT A RORSCHACH TEST??! HA HA HA!!

7-3

AND IN CONCLUSION, I HATE YOU ALL.

© 1993 United Feature Syndicate, Inc.

LET'S START WITH A BRAINSTORMING EXERCISE. ALICE, YOU GO FIRST.

I IMAGINE MYSELF NOT SURROUNDED BY DULL, UNATTRACTIVE, AND LARGELY CLUELESS MEN.

I THINK SHE JUST INSULTED YOU GUYS.

MMMM...

I'VE IDENTIFIED THE BRAIN CHEMICAL THAT CONTROLS HAPPINESS.

AND I FOUND THE EXACT MIX OF FRUIT AND VEGETABLE JUICES THAT STIMULATE ITS PRODUCTION.

DO YOU REALIZE WHAT THIS MEANS?

YEAH. FRUITS AND VEGETABLES WILL BE BANNED BY THE GOVERNMENT.

WE'RE THE GOVERNMENT. WE CAME TO CONFISCATE YOUR SO-CALLED "HAPPINESS DRUG."

IT'S NOT A DRUG! IT'S JUST A MIXTURE OF FRUITS AND VEGETABLES THAT MAKES YOU FEEL HAPPY! YOU CAN'T OUTLAW GOOD NUTRITION!

HMM... I GUESS THAT WOULDN'T MAKE SENSE, WOULD IT?

IGNORE HIM. HE'S A NEW GUY.

ERASE ALL THE FORMULAS FOR MAKING YOUR "HAPPINESS POTION" AND WE WON'T JAIL YOU.

OKAY, OKAY...

YOU CITIZENS ONLY HAVE THE RIGHT TO PURSUE HAPPINESS — YOU'RE NOT ALLOWED TO BE HAPPY.

CITIZENS NEED DISCOMFORT IN ORDER TO BE PRODUCTIVE AND FULFILLED.

WEDGIE

THEN YOU'LL LOVE THIS...

WHAT ARE YOU MAKING?

COMMEMORATIVE COLLECTIBLE PLATES.

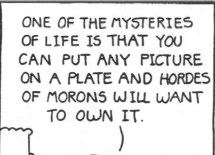

ONE OF THE MYSTERIES OF LIFE IS THAT YOU CAN PUT ANY PICTURE ON A PLATE AND HORDES OF MORONS WILL WANT TO OWN IT.

WOW! AN ACORN! AND IT'S ON A PLATE!

WHAT'S IT LIKE TO BE A MEMBER OF A HORDE?

YOU ALREADY OWN THE "ACORN SERIES" OF DOGBERT'S COMMEMORATIVE PLATES...

FOR A LIMITED TIME YOU MAY ALSO PURCHASE MY NEW ISSUE: THE "FRENCH GUY WITH A HAT" SERIES.

MY ACORN PLATES ARE MISSING.

TOMORROW I'LL INTRODUCE MY NEW SERIES: "RUSSIAN WITH FRENCH HAT."

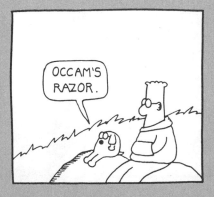

I THOUGHT OF ANOTHER WAY TO PROFIT FROM THE IGNORANCE OF HUMANS.

7-12

I WROTE "THE DOGBERT FORMULA FOR HEALTH." I RECOMMEND A DAILY DOSE OF FOOD, SLEEP AND EXERCISE.

AND FOR ONLY $19.95 YOU CAN BUY THE PATENTED "DOGBERT JOGGEROBIC CARPET PATCH" TO HELP YOU RUN IN PLACE.

© 1993 United Feature Syndicate, Inc.

ARE YOU TIRED OF FAD DIETS AND FAD EXERCISE DEVICES?

YES I AM!

7-13

THEN BUY MY BOOK AND GET THE REVOLUTIONARY JOGGEROBIC CARPET PATCH FOR ONLY $19.95 PLUS SHIPPING AND HANDLING.

TO PROVE IT WORKS, WE PHOTOGRAPHED AN ACTUAL ATHLETE.

PICTURES DON'T LIE!

© 1993 United Feature Syndicate, Inc.

IT LOOKS LIKE SALES OF THE "DOGBERT JOGGEROBIC CARPET PATCH" ARE BRISK.

YEAH, AND I'M LOOKING TO EXPAND.

7-14

RATBERT IS BUSY RESEARCHING NEW PRODUCT CONCEPTS FOR THE CARPET PATCH.

© 1993 United Feature Syndicate, Inc.

"CARPET CLUB FOR MEN."

I THINK I'VE HIT UPON A BRILLIANT NEW DIRECTION FOR EXPANDING OUR PRODUCT LINE.

7-15

I CALL THEM "CARPET PATCH KIDS." EACH ONE IS MADE FROM CARPET AND HAS ITS OWN NAME!

DON'T FEEL BAD, RAQUEL. I DON'T THINK HE MEANT IT AS A PERSONAL ATTACK.

OUR NEWEST FAD POLICY IS TO HAVE SUBORDINATES APPRAISE THEIR BOSS'S JOB PERFORMANCE.

7-16

I GIVE YOU A "D MINUS."

DID I MENTION RETRIBUTION?

CAREFUL, SIR, YOU'RE HANGING BY A THREAD.

SOMETIMES I THINK I'M NOT REACHING MY FULL POTENTIAL AS A RAT.

YOU'RE RIGHT. IN THE MIDDLE AGES, DISEASE-CARRYING RATS WIPED OUT HALF OF THE HUMAN POPULATION OF EUROPE.

I THINK I'VE GOT A LITTLE TEMPERATURE. FEEL MY FOREHEAD.

FACE IT, YOUR GLORY DAYS ARE PAST.

7-17

YOUR NEW PROJECT WILL HAVE NO BUDGET AND NO MANAGEMENT SUPPORT. EXPECT TO SPEND MOST OF YOUR TIME GIVING STATUS REPORTS.

OH NO! THE LIFE FORCE HAS BEEN DRAINED OUT OF ME! I'M BECOMING A DAMP RAG !?!

THAT'S AMAZING.

IT'S NOTHING. I DID EIGHTEEN AT ONCE AT THE EMPLOYEE EMPOWERMENT BRUNCH.

I'LL BE REPRESENTING YOU CORPORATE EMPLOYEES IN A CLASS ACTION SUIT. YOUR COMPANY HAS SUCKED THE LIFE FORCE OUT OF YOU AND TURNED YOU INTO LITTLE RAGS.

MY FEE WILL BE ON A CONTINGENCY BASIS. THAT MEANS I GET THE ENTIRE SETTLEMENT PLUS I'LL USE YOU TO WAX MY BMW.

I'VE FOUND THE PERFECT CLIENTS.

SOUNDS FAIR.

DON'T MAKE WAVES.

I'M FROM THE LAW FIRM OF DOGBERT, DOGBERT AND DOGBERT. I'M SUING YOU FOR DRAINING THE LIFE FORCE OUT OF YOUR EMPLOYEES.

AFTER BEING DRAINED OF LIFE, EMPLOYEES ARE FORCED TO LEAVE THE COMPANY. THE LUCKY ONES GET JOBS AS RAGS FOR A CAR WASH, LIKE JOEY PISHKIN HERE.

HONK HONK

WHAT JOEY? THAT'S MARGE FROM ACCOUNTING ???

THE JURY HAS REACHED A DECISION IN THE CASE OF "DOGBERT VS. A BIG CORPORATION."

WE AWARD DOGBERT FIFTY MILLION DOLLARS BECAUSE WE HATE BIG COMPANIES AND WE LIKE LITTLE DOGS WITH GLASSES.

I HATE MY LIFE.

AND WE AWARD A MAYTAG DRYER TO JUROR MINDY FOR BEING "BEST DRESSED."

DOES IT BOTHER YOU THAT I WON FIFTY MILLION DOLLARS IN MY LAWSUIT, WHEREAS YOU STILL TOIL TO REMAIN MIDDLE CLASS?

DOES IT BOTHER YOU TO KNOW THAT I COULD BUY YOU AND SELL YOU ... HOW MANY TIMES?

834 TIMES.

HEY, IT'S GONE UP SINCE LUNCH!

... SO I THOUGHT YOU MIGHT USE SOME OF YOUR NEWLY WON MILLIONS TO FUND MY "BIOWORLD" SCIENCE EXPERIMENT.

IT'S A COMPLETE ECOLOGY ENCLOSED IN AN AIRTIGHT DOME. THE SURVIVAL OF THE VOLUNTEERS WOULD DEPEND ON MY FORESIGHT AND ENGINEERING SKILLS.

GEE, I THOUGHT IT WOULD BE HARDER TO TALK YOU INTO IT.

I GET TO PICK THE VOLUNTEERS MYSELF.

I'VE COMPLETED THE DESIGN FOR BIOWORLD. HAVE YOU SELECTED THE VOLUNTEERS?

YES.

BIOWORLD

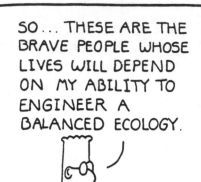

SO... THESE ARE THE BRAVE PEOPLE WHOSE LIVES WILL DEPEND ON MY ABILITY TO ENGINEER A BALANCED ECOLOGY.

SEVEN CAR SALESMEN PLUS RATBERT...

COINCIDENCE.

THE BIOWORLD DOME IS NOW SEALED. YOU MUST LIVE OFF ITS RESOURCES FOR TWO YEARS.

THE EDIBLE PLANTS WERE DELIVERED JUST BEFORE THE DOME WAS SEALED. THEY ARE THE KEY TO YOUR SURVIVAL.

CAN SOMEBODY OPEN THE DELIVERY DOOR? I'VE GOT SOME PLANTS OUTSIDE.

"DAY ONE OF THE BIOWORLD EXPERIMENT IS OFF TO A ROCKY START."

"THE VOLUNTEERS HAVE NO EDIBLE PLANTS AND THE OXYGEN LEVEL IS DROPPING."

LET US OUT

HELP

FORTUNATELY, MOST OF THE VOLUNTEERS ARE EX-CAR SALESPEOPLE, SO WE REMAIN EMOTIONALLY UNINVOLVED.

LOOK HOW THEY SPELLED "OXYGEN."

WITH OXYGEN AND FOOD NEARLY DEPLETED, THE BIOWORLD VOLUNTEERS BECOME PHILOSOPHICAL.

SOME OF THE VOLUNTEERS THINK THAT BECAUSE THEY'RE CAR SALESPEOPLE YOU DON'T VALUE THEIR LIVES...

IF THAT WERE TRUE, HOW CAN YOU EXPLAIN THAT WE PUT YOU IN THERE TOO?

THAT'S WHAT I SAID, BUT IT DIDN'T SEEM TO CHEER THEM UP.

PLEASE... END THE BIOWORLD EXPERIMENT. WE'RE OUT OF FOOD. AIR IS ALMOST GONE

WE PRAY THERE WAS NO SADISTIC INTENT WHEN YOU CHOSE ONLY CAR SALESPEOPLE FOR THE EXPERIMENT... PLEASE... AT LEAST LET SOME AIR IN...

GEE, I REALLY WANT TO HELP. I'LL GO TRY TO CONVINCE MY BOSS TO SEE IT YOUR WAY.

HEY! I'M A "SATURN" DEALER — I'M DIFFERENT!

IT USED TO BOTHER ME THAT THE AIR WAS GETTING POLLUTED AND UNBREATHABLE.

BUT I REALIZED THAT RATS ARE HARDIER THAN HUMANS — SO WE'LL GET ALL YOUR STUFF AFTER YOU WHEEZE YOUR LAST BREATH!

I THINK I'LL GO FOR A WALK.

HEY! WHY NOT DRIVE?

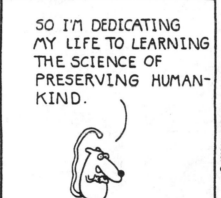

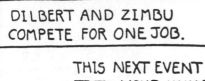

Panel 1: DILBERT AND ZIMBU COMPETE FOR ONE JOB.

THIS NEXT EVENT TESTS YOUR HUMOR AND CREATIVITY.

Panel 2: THE OBJECTIVE IS TO SEE HOW MUCH FUN YOU CAN HAVE IN THE BARREL. WHO WANTS TO GO FIRST?

8-12

Panel 3: THIS IS NO FAIR. ZIMBU IS A MONKEY. HE HAS AN ADVANTAGE.

ACTUALLY, THIS IS A TEST OF YOUR GULLIBIL-ITY.

© 1993 United Feature Syndicate, Inc.

Panel 4: AFTER COMPARING THE TWO OF YOU, I'VE DECIDED TO KEEP DILBERT FOR THE LAST ENGINEERING JOB.

8-13

Panel 5: YES! I WIN, YOU LITTLE BANANA-EATING-FLEA-HOTEL! HA HA HA HA!!!

© 1993 United Feature Syndicate, Inc.

Panel 6: I'M PUTTING ZIMBU ON THE MANAGE-MENT FAST-TRACK.

BAD TIME FOR THE VICTORY JIG.

Panel 7: DOES ANYBODY HAVE ANY QUESTIONS ABOUT OUR PLAN? ASK ME ANYTHING—THERE ARE NO "STUPID" QUESTIONS.

Panel 8: IF YOU CROSSED THE INTERNATIONAL DATE LINE ON YOUR BIRTHDAY, WOULD YOU STILL GET PRESENTS?

8-14

© 1993 United Feature Syndicate, Inc.

Panel 9: OH GREAT... THERE ARE STUPID QUESTIONS AND I DON'T KNOW THE ANSWERS.

I'M TOLD BY A RELIABLE SOURCE THAT OUR SENIOR VICE PRESIDENT MADE A SOUND LIKE "YURP" AT LUNCH.

WHAT DOES IT MEAN? DOES IT SIGNAL A NEW SET OF PRIORITIES? WE MUST DEMONSTRATE OUR COMMITMENT TO THIS VISION.

WHAT WAS THE CONTEXT OF THIS VISION?

ALL WE KNOW IS HE WAS EATING A BURRITO.

I AM DOGBERT THE PSYCHIC BUSINESS CONSULTANT. I CAN READ MINDS.

IF YOU CAN READ MINDS, WHAT'S MY FAVORITE COLOR?

YOUR FAVORITE COLOR IS PUCE, BUT YOU ARE MISTAKENLY THINKING OF A PRIMARY COLOR BECAUSE YOU DON'T KNOW WHAT PUCE IS.

WHOA... I JUST GOT A SHIVER

I WANT YOU TO READ MY BOSS'S MIND AND TELL ME WHAT HE WANTS MY GROUP TO WORK ON.

WHY DON'T YOU JUST ASK HIM?

ASK HIM?? I CAN'T DO THAT. HIS CALENDAR IS BOOKED FOR MONTHS. AND I NEVER UNDERSTAND WHAT HE SAYS ANYWAY.

HE THINKS YOU'RE AN IDIOT, BUT IT'S EASIER TO PAY YOU THAN TO FIRE YOU.

WHEW! JOB SECURITY.

369

I'M SENDING YOU TO OUR PLANT IN ELBONIA. I WANT YOU TO TEACH THEM "QUALITY."

I SELECTED YOU BECAUSE YOU'VE BEEN THERE AND YOU KNOW THEIR LANGUAGE.

THEY SPEAK ENGLISH.

OH. THEN I GUESS IT'S BECAUSE I HATE YOU.

I'LL GO WITH YOU ON YOUR TRIP TO ELBONIA. I CAN BE YOUR BODYGUARD!

IT'S NOT A GOOD PLACE FOR A RAT. THE MUD IS QUITE...

YOU THINK I'M NOT TOUGH ENOUGH? I'LL SHOW YOU!!

ELBONIA

AND THAT'S YOUR BODY-GUARD?

I DON'T LIKE THE TONE OF YOUR VOICE.

ELBONIA

I'VE BEEN SENT TO TEACH YOU "TOTAL QUALITY MANAGE-MENT."

IN THE OLD DAYS, QUALITY WAS JUST AN EMPTY WORD MEANING GOOD."

QUALITY EQUALS GOOD (1950)

EVENTUALLY IT EVOLVED INTO A COMPLICATED METHOD FOR TRANS-FERRING YOUR MONEY TO BUSINESS CONSULTANTS.

DILBERT TEACHES ELBONIA "TOTAL QUALITY" METHODS.

YOU START BY IDENTIFYING PROBLEM AREAS.

HMM... SOMETIMES OUR MITTENS GET STUCK TO OUR NOSES AND WE CAN'T BREATHE.

SNIFF

8-26

YORGI! TRY TO BREATHE WITH YOUR MOUTH!

MM! MMM!

PEOPLE! LET'S TALK METRICS, PLEASE!

© 1993 United Feature Syndicate, Inc.

DILBERT TEACHES "QUALITY" MANAGEMENT IN ELBONIA

THE FISHBONE DIAGRAM HELPS IDENTIFY THE ROOT CAUSE OF PROB-LEMS.

S. Adams

IN YOUR CASE, THE ROOT PROBLEM SEEMS TO BE THAT YOU'RE A NATION OF IMBECILES...

© 1993 United Feature Syndicate, Inc.

TRUE, BUT YOU'RE THE ONE WHO HAD TO DRAW A DEAD FISH TO FIGURE IT OUT.

YOU'RE IN THE CLUB! HERE'S YOUR HAT.

8-27

THANK YOU FOR TEACH-ING US "QUALITY" TECHNIQUES.

MANUFACTURING DEFECTS ARE DOWN FIFTY PERCENT SINCE WE ALL JOINED "QUALITY TEAMS."

YES!

S. Adams

8-28

HOW'S OUR PRODUCTIVITY, YORGI?

DOWN FIFTY PERCENT.

THEY'RE ON TO ME.

© 1993 United Feature Syndicate, Inc.

372

THIS THANKLESS ASSIGNMENT SHALL GO TO WHOEVER ASKS A QUESTION OR MAKES EYE CONTACT.

IT'S REALLY, REALLY STUPID ... DOES ANYBODY WANT TO QUESTION IT?

I THINK I SEE TED'S EYES IN THE MIRROR.

GOOD ONE, ALICE!

GASP

DO YOU REALIZE THE GOVERNMENT TAKES HALF OF ALL THE MONEY YOU MAKE?

AND THE MAJORITY OF PEOPLE ARE TOO YOUNG TO VOTE, OR DIDN'T BOTHER TO VOTE, OR VOTED FOR THE LOSER. ...AND NOBODY ALIVE VOTED FOR OUR CONSTITUTION.

IT'S NEVER GOOD WHEN YOU HAVE THESE INSIGHTS.

I'VE DECIDED TO LEVY MY OWN TAX ON PEOPLE.

HERE ARE THE DOGBERT TAX FORMS. PAY PROMPTLY OR YOU WILL BE PENALIZED.

IT'S NOT FAIR!

YOU CAN'T JUST LEVY YOUR OWN TAXES; WHAT MAKES YOU THINK I'LL PAY?

IF NOT, I'LL PUT YOU IN MY NEW PRISON.

YOU MEAN, YOU BUILT A PRISON WITH THE TAXES YOU'VE ALREADY COLLECTED?

I THINK OF IT AS "INFRA-STRUCTURE."

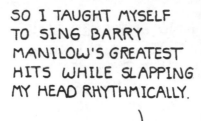

Panel 1:

DOGBERT IS HIRED AS A BLAME CONSULTANT.

THE COMPANY'S WOES ARE YOUR FAULT, NOT SENIOR MANAGEMENT'S!

9-16

Panel 2:

DO YOU REALIZE HOW MUCH YOU COULD GAIN PERSONALLY BY MAKING THE COMPANY A SUCCESS?

Panel 3:

I WOULD GET A NICE PLAQUE IN A PLASTIC FRAME.

YEAH... I WAS HOPING YOU DIDN'T KNOW.

© 1993 United Feature Syndicate, Inc.

Panel 4:

HERE'S MY CONSULTING REPORT ON YOUR COMPANY.

9-17

Panel 5:

I HAD NO INSIGHTS SO I BULKED IT UP BY ADDING WITTY ANALOGIES.

© 1993 United Feature Syndicate, Inc.

Panel 6:

"HIS HEAD WAS LIKE A HOLLOW PUTTY BALL ATTACKED BY TWO POINTY DUST BUNNIES."

VIVID, ISN'T IT?

Panel 7:

RATBERT, DID YOU KNOW THAT YOUR BRAIN AUTOMATICALLY COORDINATES MILLIONS OF ACTIVITIES EVERY SECOND?

9-18

Panel 8:

IMAGINE IF IT GOT JUST A LITTLE BIT CONFUSED — ALL THOSE NEURONS FIRING RANDOMLY...

© 1993 United Feature Syndicate, Inc.

Panel 9:

YOU DON'T ADD MUCH TO A CONVERSATION, BUT YOU'RE EASILY THE BEST LISTENER I'VE EVER MET.

AAAEE!

I BET I'VE GONE TO JAIL MORE THAN THE AVERAGE LAW-ABIDING CITIZEN.

I PLAN TO DEFEND YOU BY PROVING YOUR VICTIM WAS A TEMP WORKER.

IT'S LEGAL TO KILL A TEMP? REALLY??

NOW ALL WE NEED IS A JURY OF YOUR "PEERS."

YES, MY CLIENT DID ACCIDENTALLY SLAY A "TEMP" WORKER... EMPHASIS ON "TEMP."

BUT WHO AMONG US CAN SAY THEY HAVEN'T SLAIN INNOCENT PEOPLE WHEN THE SITUATION CALLED FOR IT?

I CAN.

WELL, GREAT... SO MUCH FOR GETTING A FAIR TRIAL.

ALTHOUGH THE INSANITY DEFENSE DOES NOT APPLY TO MY CLIENT, WE HAVE SOMETHING JUST AS GOOD.

MY CLIENT IS AN "ENGINEER SAVANT." HE UNDERSTANDS TECHNOLOGY BUT NOTHING ELSE.

AS EVIDENCE, I SUBMIT MY CLIENT'S WHITE SOCKS, COMPLETE WITH THE SOCK PROTECTOR AND AUXILIARY WRITING TOOLS.